Getting It Right
When It Matters Most

Getting It Right
When It Matters Most

Self-Leadership for Work and Life

Tony Gambill and Scott Carbonara

Leader in applied, concise business books

Getting It Right When It Matters Most: Self-Leadership for Work and Life

Cover design by Flip Design Studio, Inc.

Interior design by Exeter Premedia Services Private Ltd., Chennai, India

First published in 2021 by
Business Expert Press, LLC
222 East 46th Street, New York, NY 10017
www.businessexpertpress.com

ISBN-13: 978-1-63742-022-5 (paperback)
ISBN-13: 978-1-63742-023-2 (e-book)

Business Expert Press Business Career Development Collection

Collection ISSN: 2642-2123 (print)
Collection ISSN: 2642-2131 (electronic)

First edition: 2021

10 9 8 7 6 5 4 3 2 1

Description

Discover how to *Get It Right* in your *Moments That Matter*—when the situation is complex and relational—and the stakes are high. Transform the outcome of your most challenging situations and interactions when you feel—

- **Threatened** by charged emotions or uncertainty
- **Paralyzed** by fear of saying (or doing) the wrong thing (again)
- **Defeated** by a relationship that seems damaged beyond repair
- **Perplexed** about how to achieve the results you desire
- **Stalled** in progress with others due to differing styles and perspective

In an ever-changing environment when typical habits, behaviors, and thinking aren't enough, *Getting It Right When It Matters Most* introduces research-backed insight and a simple model for your most important situations. Apply self-awareness, learning agility, and emotional intelligence through the Self, Outlook, Action, and Reflection (SOAR) cycle.

Keywords

emotional intelligence; mindfulness; empathy; learning agility; difficult conversations; unconscious bias; perception bias; self-awareness; crucial conversations; critical conversations; listening; self-leadership; mindset; reflection; workplace drama; interpersonal conflict; conflict resolution; workplace conflict; high-stakes conversations; quality questions; perspectives; meditation; relationships

Contents

Rave Reviews for *Getting It Right When It Matters Most*

"I love when authors create simple solutions for our complicated world, and that's exactly what Tony and Scott have done here. This book jumps into the middle of all the complex situations we all face every day and provides a clear path forward. There's deep, practical wisdom in the SOAR approach." —**Jon Acuff, New York Times bestselling author of Soundtracks, The Surprising Solution to Overthinking**

"Everyone needs to read Getting It Right When It Matters Most. With their decades of knowledge and experience, Tony and Scott teach us how to get along and work with others in the face of conflicting ideologies and contrary motives. What makes this book so special is that the SOAR technique is just as effective at home as it is in the workplace." —**Bob Crawford, bassist for The Avett Brothers band, co-managing partner for the Press On Fund, and co-host for the Road to Now podcast**

"Tony and Scott provide valuable insights and a tangible action plan— SOAR—that can be effectively applied during the make-or-break professional and personal interactions we all face in life. The notion that just a small number of these key moments, and their outcomes, determine much of our success and failure in life is a critically important reality to recognize. Getting It Right empowers the reader with the ability to self-identify these crucial encounters and provides the toolkit necessary to successfully navigate them." —**Devon Godfrey, PhD, assistant professor of radiation oncology; chief editor of Advances in Medical Physics, Vols 5&6**

"In moments that matter most, this book provides a framework for getting it right. Navigating a dynamic professional landscape can tax Your Best Self and your professional relationships. Tony and Scott provide a clear path to resolve

complex problems while delicately navigating complex relationships. All too often we forget to self-reflect and SOAR brings that important practice to the forefront." —**Dr. Karen Bull, dean of the division of online learning, University of North Carolina Greensboro**

"A successful life starts with building and maintaining relationships. Getting It Right lays out the plan: how to ask questions, listen for answers, and empathize your way into the hearts of others." —**Randy Grimes, former NFL center with the Tampa Bay Buccaneers, founder of Athletes in Recovery, author of Off Center**

"Few things get done right on the first take. Film directors create the illusion of the perfect shot by editing and do-overs. In real life, though, we face certain situations when we need to get things right the first time to grow strong, positive relationships. Getting It Right shows you how to do it." —**Jennifer Gimenez, American supermodel, actress, reality television personality, and addiction recovery advocate**

"Wow!—finally something for human resource professionals to include in their learning and development programs for all employees! A real focus on driving results in business and personal life. Very impactful!" —**Kimberly Lindsay Williams, founder & CEO, North Carolina for Military Employment (NC4ME) & chief human resource officer, City of Jacksonville, North Carolina**

"If I had this book back when I transitioned from twenty-one years in the Army to my program/project management career, it could have saved me the grief of a lot of hard lessons. I can still vividly recall the many mistakes I made along the way in my moments that mattered. It would have been nice to have known all this then!" —**Ken Grant, LTC US Army (Ret); PMP certified project manager**

"Getting It Right When It Matters Most offers a profoundly timely and practical guide for self-leadership in the most challenging moments of work and personal life. Combining their own ample experience as leaders and with leaders, as well as tried and tested research insights, Tony Gambill and Scott

Carbonara distill a process for disentangling problems from noise and choosing a course of action towards a resolution that aligns with a leader's best self. A must-read for anyone wanting to take their self-leadership to a whole new level." —**Beatriz Coningham, chief people officer, Pan American Development Foundation**

"As a believer in the long-term effectiveness of self-mentoring and self-leadership, I appreciate how Getting It Right compassionately addresses issues, like complex communications, confidence, betrayal, and points out ways to establish healthy boundaries. The tools are real-world and produce positive results when applied. I like how authors Gambill and Carbonara take the reader on a journey to increased personal satisfaction with a sense of sovereignty and trust." —**Anne Bruce, bestselling author of Discover True North, Discover True North Relationships and Be Your Own Mentor, producer and host of the popular Vlog #30SecondsAtTheBeach**

"Getting it wrong is easy. This book shows you the steps required to get it right, which begins when we work on ourselves, choose healthier outlooks, and really listen to the person sitting next to us. That's when true progress begins." —**Tim Ryan, founder and executive director of A Man in Recovery Foundation, subject of the A&E special Dope Man, and author of From Dope to Hope: A Man in Recovery**

"Never be caught off guard again! This book equips you with the skills and strategies to be Your Best Self even in your worst moments." —**Marlene Chism, culture consultant, author of Stop Workplace Drama, and speaker**

"Getting It Right is an essential book for understanding how you show up and how to make meaningful adjustments to maximize your presence in any situation. What is a better gift to yourself, your family, and your work than to be Your Best Self." —**Rob Kramer, author of Stealth Coaching, CEO, executive coach, and educator**

"I knew this book would make me consider how I make decisions, but I didn't expect it to cause me to rethink some foundational aspects of *how I perceive and respond to internal and external stimuli. Since reading, I've begun to notice shifts that reframed and caused me to let go of behavior patterns that no longer serve. This is not what I was expecting, but very welcome, and I've learned new questions to guide me in the future."* —**Laura Steward, speaker, bestselling author of What Would a Wise Woman Do?, host of It's All About the Questions podcast**

"In our work and life, some days are filled with simply doing the best we can. We try, we fail, and we try again. But some days include situations that require special care: when we need to say the right thing, make the right decision, or handle a relationship in the right way. Authors Tony Gambill and Scott Carbonara call these times 'moments that matter,' and for many years they have taught leaders how to get things right in those challenging times. Drawing on their many years of experience in consulting, coaching, and counseling, the authors are now sharing their wisdom with all of us in the form of this book. Highly readable and eminently practical, Getting It Right deserves a place in the library of any leader." —**Richella Parham, speaker and author of Mythical Me: Finding Freedom from Constant Comparison**

Foreword

During unprecedented, uncertain, and often volatile moments—whether in history or in our personal and professional lives—we need a game plan more than ever. With reflection, reevaluation, and prioritization, many of us come through such challenges by acquiring a better sense of what's most important—paying that forward to our families, businesses, and communities.

In my role as a leader, consultant, and an occupational therapist, I often meet people when they're stuck, overwhelmed by injury, illness, or stressful life events for which no quick fix exists. While these challenges can happen to any of us—and our knowledge, skills, grit, passionate benevolence, and creativity will help—many lack a process for putting it all together and calling on it when faced with a real-world situation. *Getting It Right* fills the need for a research-informed, action-oriented, situationally driven game plan for the moments that matter most to our individual and collective success.

I often hear clients say, "Life is *real!*" when faced with the most complex challenges (e.g., managing organizational-level change, developing and sustaining healthy relationships, excelling in a new personal or professional role). We know that mastering these challenges—for our own success and that of our partners—calls on individuals and groups (teams, businesses, families, and communities) to strengthen their adaptive capacities and work together; but effective strategies for transforming dreams of success into real-world solutions are hard to find. *Getting It Right* with its powerful SOAR cycle is perfect for anyone who fears their challenge is insurmountable, wonders how to begin self-leadership, or still insists there's no instruction manual for life's most complex problems. So, when life gets *real* (and it will eventually), start putting all your knowledge, skills, grit, and life experiences to work in the SOAR process. Mastering the moments that matter will be the key to success, individually and as a whole.

When referring to the title *Getting It Right*, the sharper image of what "it" is (the goals and intentions we urgently want and need to pursue) begs the next question, "How will we get there?" This book closes the gap between knowing what I want and mindfully, systematically making it happen—for myself and my partners. It offers both a roadmap and a pair of wise, lighthearted tour guides who help readers *mobilize* their knowledge, skills, and valuable life experiences to realize their goals. The authors' SOAR process (complete with tips for avoiding or resetting after common mistakes) promises to help readers resolving their current challenges and becoming more adaptive and ready to tackle inevitable future challenges. Readers who are ready to SOAR need look no further than *Getting It Right When It Matters Most*.

Don't be fooled by the authors' straight-talk, humor, or talent for storytelling. A deeper insight into Gambill and Carbonara's indispensable, tested and proven, collective wisdom arrives in the intro, when they explain that discrete skills taught in other books (e.g. mindfulness practices or communication strategies) are inadequate for resolving real-world problems, and *Getting It Right* is the first book to put it all together with a comprehensive cycle that you can apply to any situation that is important, complex, and relational. No other leadership experts are more qualified than these two when it comes to leading readers through the critical (and totally do-able) process of understanding one's Self, choosing your best Outlook, selecting the right Actions, and engaging in meaningful Reflection for growth (SOAR). What makes *Getting It Right* such a fun read is that it's not only for the once-in-a-lifetime scenario its title implies. Instead, it's as much an everyday game plan—improving with practice and discovery—as a real-world, high-stakes strategy from two deeply informed, intrepid, and passionate leadership coaches who are still in the game.

—M. Heather McKay, PhD, OT/L, founder of Partnerships for Health www.pfhnc.com

Dr. McKay is an occupational therapist, dementia care specialist, and international trainer/speaker on topics related to dementia care and caregiver education

Acknowledgments

The authors would like to thank their families for their patience, love, and support while they labored to bring this book to the world. They promise to make it up to you now that it is finished.

Additionally, they extend a personal thank you to Jocelyn Carbonara for her developmental editing and project management over the entire book writing process.

Finally, Tony and Scott wish to thank every boss, peer, and employee they have been privileged to work with throughout the years, especially in those moments when the authors did not Get It Right.

Introduction

It's not about being right. It's about getting it right.

—Elizabeth Spelke

Ninety percent of your life is spent saying and doing the right things without a second thought. You do not need to think. Your core intelligence, manners (refined by years of practice), and good old-fashioned "people skills" take over, navigating you expertly through or around almost every scenario you encounter.

We did not write this book to help you *Get It Right* when the situation is simple and straightforward. You have likely already mastered those skills. And even if you have not, not every situation requires perfection or your best version of Self.

When a Situation Becomes a Moment That Matters

But some situations bring higher stakes. Depending on how they play out, these situations can turn catastrophic—or catalyzing—for your personal or professional success and even for the larger causes you serve. They may secure—or destroy—your relationships and outcomes. These situations *do* require your best.

If you leave them to the whim of chance or a habitual reaction, you may never achieve your desired goals or initiate positive change. In fact, you may sabotage those efforts.

Because of the huge potential in these situations, we refer to them as Moments That Matter (MTMs). For purposes of this book, MTMs are situations that are:

- Important (the outcome matters to your well-being or success)
- Complex (there is no simple solution)
- Relational (the situation involves at least one other person)

MTMs often involve *opportunities*—situations that, if navigated well, can bring greater success.

Think of your annual appraisal, an opportunity to showcase your performance and possibly advance your career. You cannot expect a favorable, glowing review unless you have managed to Get It Right When It Matters Most throughout the year. And, you likely cannot expect a future promotion if you blow a fuse and tell off your boss during your review (another MTM).

Or consider a broader issue—like initiating social change. As political and ideological biases may incite conflict, how can you influence outcomes, navigating differences to constructively take collective action?

Other opportunities might include developing relationships with your soon-to-be in-laws or the stakeholders of a project you oversee. For some of us, our greatest opportunities lie in the form of repetitive issues that always seem to end with the same bad results. We cannot expect to achieve different results until we find a way to Get It Right in our MTMs.

We wrote this book to help you take control and Get It Right—when autopilot is not enough. This book will help you identify, prepare for, and successfully navigate MTMs—bringing Your Best Self forward to initiate positive change.

What We Have Here is an MTM!

Fred is a manager with a midsized, Midwest manufacturing company. Fred's wife begged him for weeks to "put in a good word" for her brother Kevin at the plant. Fred finally agreed to take Kevin's resume to human resources.

Kevin got hired into another department working for Annette, and that is when Fred's real troubles began. Kevin proved unreliable, showing up late twice during his first week and missing a day without calling in sick the week after. When Kevin showed up, his performance was poor to average at best.

Yesterday, Annette marched into Fred's office.

"You really stuck me with Kevin. What were you thinking? Should I try to get *my* dead-beat brother-in-law hired and have *him* work in your area?" Annette said in a huff.

This situation was complex, lacking any clear solution. The outcome was important to Fred's reputation at work and his personal well-being, as he recommended Kevin. Finally, it was relational. Kevin's performance put Fred between the rock of his wife and the hard place of his peer and organization.

How Fred handled this situation mattered to his present and future. This was an MTM!

Beyond Personal

As this book was being written, the COVID-19 pandemic hit, highlighting vast differences in approaches, values, experiences, and perspectives. Months later, the United States responded to the tragic death of George Floyd, spurring protests and even riots. Then, the 2020 United States' presidential election brought forth further division and critical unrest. Leaders at multiple levels faced multiple and ongoing MTMs in handling the responses, policies, and communication around these situations.

How can we navigate bigger issues that are important, complex, and relational—and inform the solution? Equipping ourselves to be part of a change starts with applying the self-leadership principles in this book.

To discover if this book is right for you, read the following situations, and ask yourself if any of them sound familiar. Take note of any you have experienced in the last six months.

- When discussing important issues with others who have strong and differing opinions, do you feel ill-equipped to engage in productive, quality conversations?
- Does your first response to a negative, unplanned conflict during a crisis sometimes bring out the worst instead of the best of you?
- Do you wish you could be part of the solution to the problem instead of a bystander or instigator?

- Do you have the same arguments with the same people, only to suffer the same consequences: strained relationships and a failure to hit your goals?
- During your most challenging situations, have your emotions hijacked your clarity and decision-making?
- Do you function as a superstar individual performer, but recognize that your work success is increasingly dependent on your relationships and the actions of others?
- Is your profession experiencing major changes, and the way you have always done things is no longer sufficient to guarantee your ongoing success?
- Do you ever look back on situations and regretfully say, *I wish I had said* or *I wish I had done* things differently?
- Do you find yourself "writing off" people who are important to your success, because you can never find a way to work things out with them?
- Do you often dread people or situations that may put you out of your comfort zone?

If you have answered "yes" to any of these (and most of us have), you can benefit from this book. Given enough time, it only takes a small, unattended leak to sink a boat. Put that boat into a storm, and the leak will grow—increasing the speed of its demise.

First Thought Wrong

Comedian Mark Lundholm has a live routine called "First Thought Wrong." In difficult situations, our first response is often the wrong one. Consider the driver who cuts you off. Your first thought is likely not, *Oh, I hope he's okay; he's in such a rush.* It's probably shorter, maybe even four letters with an accompanying hand gesture. Discard that thought, and do not act on it. We will tell you how later! (See www .marklundholm.com for info on this speaker and comedian.)

You have no doubt come across buzzwords like *emotional and social intelligence* and *learning agility.* But do you know how to keep your mind clear and balanced during chaos? Do you stay calm when your emotions scream for reaction? Do you offer clarity and insight even in challenging situations? Do you maintain or even build productive relationships in moments of conflict? Do you learn quickly in real time by adapting new skills, behaviors, and beliefs? Do you navigate the ship, even when it is being battered by waves twice its size? Do you recognize how you cannot necessarily change the reaction of someone else—or solve the issue at hand—without first addressing your own biases and responses?

- Some books may teach you how to manage your emotions using mindfulness best practices. *This concept is not new.*
- Other books detail how to have complex conversations with others who are important to your success. *This concept is also well established.*
- *No other book* puts it all together. We will help you to understand Self, choose your best Outlook, select the right Actions, and engage in meaningful Reflection for growth— through a comprehensive cycle that you can apply to any situation that is important, complex, and relational. We will teach you the self-leadership skills you need to Get It Right!

Why SOAR?

Getting It Right When It Matters Most will engage you in the SOAR (Self, Outlook, Action, Reflection) cycle to get to your best destination efficiently and effectively—with all the key players still on board.

As coauthors, we bring more than 50 years of developing people and helping them navigate change. Through coaching, counseling, and training thousands in their most complex work and life opportunities, we noted that these folks came from different backgrounds and were trained in diverse professions.

We spent thousands of hours asking questions and listening to what made these people tick. Their success seemed less tied to the number of training classes they attended, their intelligence quotients (IQs), or their personality types. Those who Got It Right shared a pattern of foundational behaviors upon which all their other actions were built. These behaviors always served them well but were most evident during their most important, complex, and relational situations. In other words, *in their MTMs, these people tended to Get It Right more often than everyone else.*

We have witnessed firsthand the skills that define and separate these high-potential people. Even if they are not already where they want to be, we have seen how those who develop the practical truths in this book have increased influence along with career and personal success.

By tapping into our professional experience working with some of the most well-known organizations—and standing on the shoulders of the world's best research—we will share what these people do differently, so you can apply these lessons to your MTMs. We developed the SOAR cycle for self-leadership to help you do just that—SOAR instead of sink—in your MTMs.

Research shows that applying the actionable skills we teach in your MTMs will help you become:

- *Higher performing* in boundary-spanning jobs that require *sensitivity to social cues*
- More effective at *resolving conflicts* through *collaboration* and *compromise*
- More likely to be seen as a *transformational leader*
- Perceived as more *interpersonally competent*
- A recipient of *more promotions*

In addition, these skills will help you in life outside of your career to foster:

- Closer relationships and improved communication with the people you care about most
- Increased tolerance for ambiguous situations

Are you ready to:

- increase your skills in navigating challenging, important situations more effectively?
- improve your personal and professional effectiveness?
- expand your emotional awareness to increase your agility in real time?
- take your leadership skills to the next level?

Are you ready to *Get It Right When It Matters Most?*

CHAPTER 1

Getting It Right

Knowledge is of no value unless you put it into practice.

—Anton Chekov

We Do Not Always Get It Right at Work

Tim was pretty excited about his upcoming performance review. Not only had he exceeded most of his key goals with flying colors, but he had also volunteered for a few corporate teams, even signing up for a big role in an important charity fundraiser.

Yeah, it's been a pretty good year, Tim reminded himself as he popped his head into his boss's empty office promptly at 9:00 a.m., as scheduled. While waiting, Tim allowed himself to ponder how much of a raise he would soon be given. *Maybe I'll even be upgraded from a cubicle to a real office—one with a door*—he smiled to himself.

After about five minutes, Tim's boss Stella arrived—apologizing that her last meeting had gone late. Tim and Stella engaged in brief small talk and pleasantries before Stella leaned back in her chair, inhaling deeply before beginning her next words.

"I've conducted eight of these quarterly review sessions already this week," Stella started, as Tim leaned forward in his chair. "But," she continued, "Yours is by far the most difficult one I have on my plate."

Tim's body suddenly felt heavy as he sank in his seat. Shocked, he caught only snippets of phrases like "incomplete tasks," "too much time on non-essential projects instead of doing your primary work," and even "chronic lateness." He felt his blood pressure rising. His face turned red, as his palms got sweaty. He was trying to listen, but his body was reacting even before his words.

Tim might not have known it at the time, but he was experiencing an MTM.

Finally, Tim had heard enough and spoke up.

"Hold on a minute," he said, thrusting his hand into a stop position. "This is coming out of nowhere. I don't know how you can see it that way," Tim raised his voice defensively.

"Tim, I'm not saying that you didn't work hard. But it's not about hard work. It's about results. And sometimes, it's just doing the little things— like having 100 percent of your deliverables on time, every time," Stella answered calmly.

"*I* was on time for this meeting," Tim heard himself say before he could stop the words from spilling out of his mouth.

The meeting went downhill from there.

Later at his desk, Tim feared that he had just committed job suicide. And if that were the case, he doubted that Stella would give him a good reference to quietly change departments or find another job outside of the company.

Tim was caught off guard. He was prepared for praise, but instead he received criticism that he deemed unfair. As a result, Tim's emotions turned hot and he raised his voice. Finally, he popped and said something he could not find a way to take back.

Why am I such an idiot? Tim asked himself, reflecting on his words and actions.

We Do Not Always Get It Right at Home

As Thanksgiving approached, Grace was filled with dread at the thought of hosting the family holiday dinner at her home. Grace loved family, but she did not like what happened when her brother-in-law Gary picked fights, which seemed to happen at every gathering.

Grace could not understand Gary's lack of etiquette. Hadn't he heard that polite people avoid the three taboo topics of money, religion, or politics? Instead of making those subjects off-limits, those were the only topics Gary seemed interested in discussing at length. And because the upcoming national election grew more heated and ugly as election day approached, she envisioned the dining room table as the platform for Gary to hold a rally, protest, and counter-protest all in one.

So, Grace wasn't surprised at Thanksgiving when the fireworks started right away. Gary's booming voice bellowed before his body ever cleared the front door.

"Who's driving that little wind-up toy with the Communist bumper stickers on it?" Gary asked.

Gary had fought with valor in the Vietnam War and recently retired as the lead technician at a large plumbing company.

Grace did not know it, but she, too, was experiencing an MTM.

Grace took a deep breath and muttered to her husband, Steve, "The fascist is here."

"Be kind, Grace," Steve soothed. "Gary was a war hero."

Popping his head into the kitchen, Gary asked loudly, "Please tell me you didn't make a gluten-free, dairy-free, sugar-free, vegan meal, did you?"

"I would have," Grace muttered under her breath, "If that would have made this holiday Gary-free."

The petty jabs and snide comments continued until the last guest left the home.

Lying in bed that night, Grace's mind replayed the day. *Why does this happen every time Gary and I get in the same room?* She asked in the darkness. By the end of dinner, Grace had felt physically exhausted, with her opinions unchanged and her feelings hurt. *Why does this keep happening? Is it me? Is it Gary?*

You Are Not Alone

Nobel Prize winning psychologist Daniel Kahneman famously claimed that we each experience about 20,000 moments in a waking day, most lasting only a few seconds (Rath and Clifton 2020). We have all experienced moments at home and work when we knew immediately that we missed a chance to say things we wish we had. Or perhaps more troubling, we say things that later make us cringe.

These moments are typically wrapped into larger situations, ones where we knowingly repeat the same mistakes over and over again, unaware of other options available to us.

If you have had regrets, there is likely nothing wrong with your DNA or intelligence. Nor were your parents or society remiss for not teaching you manners and social skills. As evidence, the authors offer this simple question, "Don't you Get It Right most of the time?" Of course, you do. It just does not *feel* that way.

Almost all of the memorable moments you can recall at the end of each day could be put in one of two buckets: positive or negative.

Of the two buckets, guess which ones you are most likely to recall? Psychologist Dr. Rick Hanson explains that our minds are "like Velcro for negative experiences, but Teflon for positive ones," meaning that you will always find it easier to recall negative events—like the times you said the wrong things or thought of the right things too late—than positive events or the many times you *got it right*. The term for our human tendency to let negative events stick and positive events to get forgotten is called a *negativity bias* (Hanson 2016).

If you are like most people, your habits serve you well 90 percent of the time, but it is the 10 percent that keeps you awake at night. And, thanks to the wiring of your brain, you likely recall your failures much more readily than your victories.

Knowledge Is Not Enough

For more than four decades, we have led thousands of leaders and professionals interested in growth through the most cutting-edge, rigorous, accurate personality assessments ever created, teaching them how to better understand themselves and others. We have also shown leaders how they were perceived by others, giving them one-on-one coaching and feedback from their peers, direct reports, managers, and key stakeholders. In the classroom, we have shared the latest leadership research to maximize effective behaviors and minimize nonproductive ones.

Those attending our training sessions had several things in common. Most of them possessed:

- *Intelligence.* Think physicians, nurses, scientists, researchers, project managers, chief executive officers (CEOs), chief information officers (CIOs), chief human resource officers

(CHROs), leaders of federal agencies, and even a few actual rocket scientists. In tough financial times, the first thing most companies cut is employee training. But organizations always manage to fund learning for their top leaders and performers.

- *Solid understanding of their own personalities and preferences.* They also obtained a deep understanding of the impact of their actions and behaviors on those they led.
- *Great intentions.* They wanted to do the right thing for the business and by others.
- *A willingness and eagerness.* They wanted to put what they learned to immediate use.

Sadly, many of them had one more thing in common: once outside of the classroom, most got caught up in the speed and complexity of their respective roles and *reverted to their old ways of doing things!*

People can and do learn skills and acquire knowledge. They gain self-awareness about their strengths and weaknesses, styles, and preferences—to a point. People usually do not fail because they lack intelligence, time-on-job, knowledge of the right people, personality type, genetic makeup, communication style, problem-solving, delegation, coaching, or any other single element taught in a training class.

People fail when typical habits, reactions, behaviors, and thinking are not enough, and a situation calls for them to bring their best resources forward. When times are tough, many struggle to relate to others and adapt new thinking and actions to drive success.

Some Moments—and Relationships—Matter More Than Others

Remember Grace? She tossed and turned all night. Wanting to keep peace in the family and repair her relationship with Gary, she spent most of the night thinking about how she wished she had responded differently.

What Grace experienced in bed that night is called *esprit de l'escalier*, a uniquely French phrase (yet culturally universal phenomenon) meaning "that thing you wish you had said in the moment...*but didn't.*"

What Tim experienced after his performance review is expressed best by another French phrase known as a *faux pas*, "that thing you said and *wished immediately you hadn't.*"

We have all experienced *esprit de l'escalier* and *faux pas* moments.

While not every moment requires you to show up with our best version of yourself, some do. Not every faux pas causes the same amount of damage as other mistakes. But, some create great harm. And, what you say and do in those moments might change the direction of your career or relationships with others moving forward.

What Do We Mean by Moments That Matter?

Building on Daniel Kahneman's research about how people experience about 20,000 individual moments each day, Researcher Timothy D. Wilson of the University of Virginia claims that we have 11 million pieces of information entering our brains within any given moment (Wilson 2004). If we have 11 million pieces of information bombarding our 20,000 moments, each day, we are flooded with 220,000,000,000 pieces of data! While Wilson concludes that we can only be conscious (on our best days) of about 40 pieces of data in any given moment, that is still quite a lot of information to sift through.

The good news is, you do not have to act on those 220,000,000,000 bits of data, nor do the vast majority of those data points matter. And, of the 20,000 moments you experience each day, only a small portion of those really matter.

But some MTMs matter greatly to your well-being and success.

In fact, some moments have a profound impact. Think about those moments that make your heart race, leave your palms sweaty, and release butterflies into your stomach. Maybe you lie in bed at night anticipating these moments or rehashing them after they occur. You walk away playing the scenario over in your head, wondering if you got it right—or worse, fearing that you got it wrong. Maybe you said something you regretted—or did not say something and wish you had. MTMs can either be spontaneous, one-off situations or ongoing situations with a person or a group of people.

MTMs Have Three Traits

1. **Important, with an outcome that matters to your well-being or success.**

   From Grace's perspective, her own political views were correct, and Gary's were wrong. She considered her opinions as facts and Gary's as just plain silly. As much as she reminded herself that she wanted to get along, she struggled with letting Gary spout lies as truths without at least trying to set the record straight! The outcome mattered, because it had the potential to create a divide—or unity—in the family. That outcome could potentially last for generations.

   When it came to Tim's review, Stella might have blown it by focusing on the negatives upfront. But Tim did not control his emotions, something that would come back to haunt him. Tim viewed himself as successful, and he reviewed his year as one of great accomplishment. How could he just "let it go" and move forward?

2. **Complex, with no simple solution.**

   Grace understood that were she to continue fighting with her brother-in-law, she would get what she has always gotten: more resentment and hard feelings. Were she to stop talking to Gary or refuse to attend any family function when Gary was present, she would miss out on many opportunities to enjoy the rest of her family. She saw no simple answer.

   Tim found himself in a similar position. He entered his appraisal meeting with excitement but left with frustration and dread. Had he stayed silent, he would signal to Stella that he understood and agreed with her—neither of which was true. But, by responding the way he did, he sounded petty. He did not know how to Get It Right in his MTM, and he would not sleep well until he figured out what to do next.

3. **Relational, involving at least one other person.**

   Grace loved her family, needed them in her life, desired a close relationship, and wanted to consider their needs. She would rather have crotchety Gary arguing in her home than a peaceful home without him. She started thinking a better relationship with Gary might begin with herself. But how?

Tim's relationship with Stella was crucial too. Stella could discipline, promote, or sabotage Tim's ability for future success. Tim's success, by anyone's definition, was based on Stella's opinion. What could he do differently next time?

In MTMs, we choose how to initiate a conversation or respond to someone's behavior or words. We can create meaningful dialogue, lasting change, and substantial growth. Or, we can damage relationships and ensure future growth is stunted.

Consider a couple of your present (or recent) MTMs. In what situations do you historically struggle to Get It Right? Document a couple in Table 1.1 that repeat themselves or that you face today. Then, describe what makes them important, complex, and relational. Finally, write down your desired outcome.

Table 1.1 MTM breakdown

Describe MTM	How is it *important?*	How is it *complex?*	How is it *relational?*	Desired outcome

You may find it helpful to reference these MTMs as you read on, to help you develop strategies and apply tips to *Getting It Right When It Matters Most*.

Positive Psychology: The Study of What Works

Unlike traditional psychology that focuses on shrinking problems, positive psychology focuses on applying what works. If you want to know how to live a long life, study those who have made it to 100. What did they do differently? Can you learn from their habits?

As practitioners of positive psychology, we didn't write this book as a primer on how to Get It Wrong—but on how to Get It Right. We spotlight what to do differently to secure better outcomes.

Success is not just the absence of failure—but the presence of the right behaviors and mindset. We will share those best practices with you!

Do You Get It Right?

Read through the following situations and anticipate your natural, immediate reaction:

- You walk in on a work celebration for your newly promoted coworker who took *your* idea to your joint-boss and got promoted for it. *It matters.*
- Your boss presented you a great development opportunity to lead a strategic project completely outside of your area of experience, and you lack the internal relationships to succeed in it. *It matters.*
- As you enter your home, your spouse starts a conversation showing you that *clearly* you are about to have a heated, all-night argument. *It matters.*
- Your most important customer says your organization is not delivering enough and they are looking for a new vendor. *It matters.*
- You received a big promotion and you are now managing your former peers. *It matters.*
- Approaching the kitchen, you hear your teenaged son cursing at his mother as he gestures threateningly. *It matters.*
- Your new boss has an entirely new strategy for future success and you do not believe she sees you as part of the solution. *It matters.*
- Your success on a key project is dependent on successful collaboration with a coworker, who is not delivering their part. *It matters.*
- After being separated from your spouse for six months, your 10-year-old daughter gets called into the principal's office for being sent to school by your ex in a skirt that is too short.

While there, you discover that your ex also did not pack her a lunch or send lunch money. Last week, your ex failed to sign a field trip permission slip. As you are listed first on the school's call list, you are having to deal with this—again. *It matters.*

- You scroll through social media and notice that someone you thought of as a close friend posted an article with what you consider incorrect information based on political biases. You could block or hide this person online, but you also have to work together on a community project. You stay up all night, scripting responses in your head. *It matters.*

- As protests erupt around a racially charged shooting, your coworker continues to make comments that make you feel uncomfortable. *It matters.*

- As a public health crisis emerges, you and your spouse differ in your approaches on how to keep your family safe. *It matters.*

- After months working long hours on a difficult cross-divisional team project, a manager from another department goes to your boss, asking that you be replaced because "you're difficult to work with." *It matters.*

- You wake up on a Saturday morning to the sound of your new neighbor taking a chainsaw to your tree on the property line. (By the way, this situation happened to Scott.) *It matters.*

The *outcome of each of these examples is important.* Each is *complex,* offering no easy resolutions. And, each involves a *relationship with some-one else.* These are MTMs. Thinking later about "what I should have said" will not help, and a faux pas on your part may well make matters worse. What do you do?

Skills for Finding Clarity in Ambiguity

We all come across important moments we are not prepared for, when we have no previous experience or classroom education to guide us.

Sometimes, this involves an *outside change or crisis* that rocks our current way of doing things. As this book was being finished, the authors experienced the beginning of the COVID-19 crisis, which changed daily routines and challenged nearly everyone. Routine changes can include a new information technology (IT) system, regulatory mandates, or mergers.

Sometimes, the ambiguity comes from a *relationship or personal situation* we do not know how to navigate—such as a new boss, political conflict with someone at work, or a family member doing something we wish they would stop.

You undoubtedly experience times when—

- You have no clear answer about what to say or do
- You feel threatened and afraid of doing the wrong thing
- You have already said the wrong thing and face a damaged relationship
- The relationship seems impossible to maintain or repair
- Your emotions are hijacked, making you more likely to act in a way that will sabotage your results
- You know the results you want but do not see any good options

We often run head-on or, even worse, are blindsided by these situations. What can you do instead? How can you rise above and not be a slave to the moment? If you struggle during these MTMs or do not feel equipped to navigate the stormy seas, then this book is for you.

Dr. Martin Luther King Jr. said, "The ultimate measure of a man is not where he stands in moments of comfort and convenience, but where he stands at times of challenge and controversy." These are the critical times in your career and life. These are the times when it matters how you show up. These are the moments that define your career, and more importantly, your life.

Entering the SOAR Cycle

Our successes or setbacks are directly tied to how we show up when engaging with our MTMs. These moments have a rhythm and flow—meaning they do not need to occur chaotically, if you recognize and plan for them.

Figure 1.1 The SOAR cycle

We have organized the four phases of that rhythm to include: Self, Outlook, Action, and Reflection (we will use the acronym SOAR). We will touch on each of them briefly here and then in much more detail throughout this book.

For better or worse, you bring Self to every *MTM* you encounter, which creates a need for an intentional Outlook that allows you to choose one or a set of Actions—that lead to either positive, negative, or neutral Reflection. That is the cycle.

In fact, SOAR is a cycle that you go through hundreds of times each day without giving it much thought, and rightfully so as you would not ever get anything done if you always needed to slow down before taking action.

Let us explore a very simple example, which may require a stretch to meet the litmus test of being important to our success, but it does involve a *relationship* and *situation that could be deemed as complex* (depending on the family dynamic and history).

Let us say your 16-year-old son asks you if he can go play video games with his friend down the block.

- Your Self (what you bring to the table) has been presented an MTM that you may not even recognize.
- You can either say "yes" or "no," depending on your Outlook (lens for seeing this situation).
- You choose the Action to say "no."
- But you are not done. You then enter a Reflection stage when your son says a few nasty words, stomps upstairs, and slams his door. And then, you spend the next several hours wondering if you made the right decision.

This is a simple example of how we continually go through the SOAR cycle and do not need to give much additional thought to the how, what, and why we did it this way. This is a common and straightforward situation.

Or is it? Let us add some complexity that can turn this almost non-event into something bigger:

- Maybe your son has struggled to make new friends since your family moved into the area nine months ago. So you considered saying "yes."
- Maybe you have hours of work ahead of you, so you considered saying "yes" just to have a quiet home.
- Maybe your son, who regularly makes C grades, has worked very hard since the beginning of the school year, so you wanted to say "yes" to reward him.
- Maybe you have been closely following the strong recommendations from the Centers for Disease Control and Prevention (CDC) to practice social distancing until the COVID-19 crisis passes its peak. So you know you have to say "no."

The MTM might happen before you walk in the door. You show up tired and hungry. You had a bad day. Or, on the flip side, you just got a promotion. You got great sleep the night before and you are looking forward to a weekend with as few kids as possible around!

We will explore more about this cycle and your MTMs through-out this book. But it is easy to see how even simple situations can have complex components—and become opportunities to Get It Right.

The Journey Begins

In the following chapters, we provide the knowledge and tools to effectively manage Self, bring awareness and clarity to your opportunities through your Outlook, create insights for the best Actions, and under-stand and learn from your results through Reflection.

Through it all, you will be taught the skills that make a difference in your MTMs—skills that help you SOAR instead of sink.

And here is how we are going to do it. Have you ever wondered how first responders (police, nurses, doctors, emergency medical technicians (EMTs), firemen, etc.) act with such skill during moments of life and death? First, they do not learn new skills in the middle of a real life and death crisis. You would not drop a new firefighter into the middle of a wildfire and expect a good, safe outcome for the firefighter, her colleagues, or the public. Rather, first responders are taught small, precise skills in a safe environment away from the chaos of an actual crisis until they can act without thinking, instead depending on muscle memory and habit.

Second, successful first responders learn to slow down chaotic, dan-gerous situations. Researchers refer to this "slowing down of time" as *time dilation*. Cognitive neuroscientists have found that baseball players at bat, for example, describe that time slows down and visual information increases when they face a fastball at home plate—allowing them to hit a ball that most eyes are not trained to track!

First responders who are properly trained and operating according to the oaths they took do the same thing, slowing down time to understand, assess, and act with precision in the face of life-threatening situations. (Those who do not slow down time to respond instead of react may make dangerous or deadly decisions.)

Similarly, in the chapters that follow, we will slow down each phase of the SOAR cycle to teach you how to best navigate your MTMs in a "safe environment." You will learn self-leadership tools to apply in real time and understand how to avoid common traps that prevent you from Getting It Right.

PART I

Self

The SOAR cycle—Self

CHAPTER 2

Me, Myself, and I

True nobility lies in being superior to your former self.
—Ernest Hemingway

In Chapter 1, we briefly described our self-leadership SOAR cycle. We promised to slow down the cycle so that we can illustrate the knowledge and tools you need to effectively navigate MTMs. Let's explore how slowing down the process works.

Preparing One's Self for the High Seas

Scott's wife, Jocelyn, once chartered a small sailboat from Florida to the Bahamas. Her "Uncle Paul" captained it and allowed Jocelyn to bring four friends as crew. As Uncle Paul was the only experienced sailor, he sent the rest of the crew homework to read and terms to learn—including parts of the boat and how to tie a proper knot.

Once they arrived in Florida, after loading and boarding the boat, the crew didn't head straight to the open sea. Instead, they navigated down the intracoastal waterway to practice their skills and learn their roles. They tested hoisting the sails and taking them down, turning the boat around, issuing commands, activating the radio, harnessing into their safety lines, and plotting their course.

The new crew developed the foundational skills needed to keep them safe and moving toward their desired destination. They didn't learn random, irrelevant strategies; instead, they spotlighted knowledge and skills they most needed before heading out to the high seas. By practicing as the sun shone and water reflected like glass—with EMTs and boat mechanics nearby in case of a major mistake—they prepared for the test ahead. (They even steered into the ocean briefly, where two of them "practiced" getting seasick!) At sunset, the crew decided it was time to cross the Gulf Stream.

Similar to the sailing crew practicing skills before hitting the pressure of the high seas, if you desire to reach your destination in your MTM with more success, you will need to master the Self you bring into those situations—before they occur. The skills you learn in this Self phase will be *crucial* to making the most of each MTM that comes your way. Through Self leadership, you can contribute your best to accomplish a shared goal.

We will revisit the crew's sailing journey in each section of the book, as we address how to SOAR and not sink in your MTMs. Like a sailing crew SOARing through the water, we want to help you navigate challenges with all the skills you need to get to your destination—with your relationships intact.

What Do We Mean by Self?

The first online dictionary definition we found is as good as any—

Self / *noun*

noun: **self**; plural noun: **selves**

a person's essential being that distinguishes them from others, especially considered as the object of introspection or reflexive action.

Having assessed thousands of individuals on intelligence quotient (IQ) tests, emotional intelligence (EQ) assessments, and personality inventories such as Myers Briggs, The Achiever, DiSC, and so on, we will admit that we are nerds. Each of these assessments takes a picture of the same individual, just at a slightly different angle. We've come to believe the knowledge learned from tools such as these, while interesting and relevant, doesn't always promote growth. Nor do they tell the full story of Self, much like how a photograph shows only one angle of a face. We are complex, and each situation elicits different thoughts, intentions, and behaviors. Life is dynamic.

For the purpose of SOAR, think of Self as the real, unique you that has evolved over time based on your one-of-a-kind combination of:

- Memories
- Experiences
- Personality
- Physical traits
- Tendencies
- Habits
- Intelligence
- Beliefs
- Preferences
- Strengths
- Weaknesses
- Assumptions

Self-Awareness: Who Are You?

Before unwrapping the concept of Self, we need to begin with how aware you are of what makes you *you*. We call this self-awareness.

Adrian Furnham defines self-awareness as "the accurate appraisal and understanding of your abilities and preferences and their implications for your behavior and impact on others" (*How to Develop Self-Awareness* 2017).

Simply put, you have self-awareness if you know why you *do what you do* and *think what you think*. Self-awareness involves knowing your true character, what motivates you, what drives your feelings, and what fuels your desires. When mindful of whether your thoughts and emotions lift you up or bring you down, you can adjust as necessary.

Without self-awareness—when you don't know why you do or think the things that you do, what motivates you, how your feelings move you forward or slow you down, and what fuels your desires—any important, complex, and relational situation can quickly become overwhelming.

> *Everything that irritates us about others can lead us to an understanding of ourselves.*
>
> —Carl Gustav Jung

Imagine responding to the doctor who asks, "Where does it hurt?" with, "I have no idea." Self-awareness allows you to perform an ongoing *diagnostic* of what is working well or what needs to improve.

Everyone Has Self-Awareness, Right?

Babies are born with a delightful lack of self-awareness, remaining blissfully clueless that anyone might have an agenda that differs from their own. When a baby fills her diaper, she feels no embarrassment. When she screams all night before your big meeting with the boss, she offers no apologies. Were you and your partner to discuss the need for continuous birth control moving forward, your baby takes no offense. Babies are incapable of showing the slightest bit of jealousy, embarrassment, shame, envy, or empathy, which is kind of refreshing.

It's much less refreshing when you see those same characteristics in your spouse, boss, coworker, or the mirror. Do you know someone who is equally clueless about social or professional norms? Think of that neighbor who walks his dog across the street to relieve itself on *your* lawn. Could you imagine the person sitting next to you in church saying "boring!", loudly and clearly, while the minister is talking? Or an uninvited guest walking into your business meeting to grab a cup of coffee and a donut off the table?

Sure, we might fantasize about doing some of those things, but self-awareness and an understanding of social norms tend to keep our behavior in check.

Babies start developing self-awareness around the 15- to 24-month mark. Using the "rouge test," a mom will place a dab of red rouge on her child's nose and then sit that child in front of a mirror. Prior to 15 months of age, a baby might look at his own reflection but not recognize himself or realize that the red dot is on his own nose. But, starting around 15 months, a baby will look in the mirror and make a great discovery: "Hey! I know that guy!" Furthermore, at around that age, when a baby sees a red dab of rouge on his nose, he realizes the dot is not on the reflection but on his own nose!

Have you ever watched an infant make the discovery for the first time that he has the power to move his hand or foot? Before that moment, the child would wiggle and move, but any limb that crossed his eyes seemed as random as looking at the night sky just in time to see a shooting star.

But then, it happens! Awareness enters the child's mind that the hand up in the air is *his* hand, and the foot overhead is *his* foot. And, for the time being, the child has a new friend: a hand or foot that can provide hours of endless entertainment!

From that moment on, we constantly gather more self-awareness—and learn that we are unique and independent from the next person. As we grow and mature, we realize we control so much more than just our limbs. We own our thoughts, attitudes, and actions every moment.

Over time and experience, we develop values, personality, emotions, strengths, and weaknesses. The more we understand ourselves, the more we gain control over how we think and feel—and eventually what we do. We learn how to motivate ourselves, manage our stress, and make better decisions. And, if we serve as leaders, high self-awareness allows us to connect with others to lead them more effectively.

Our level of self-awareness varies, but there are steps we can take to increase it.

Why We Need Self-Awareness

Why would we want to increase our self-awareness?

The benefits of self-awareness are well documented. Multiple research studies support that self-awareness informs better outcomes in decision-making, skill development, adaptation to change, as well as interpersonal and communication skills—all leading to higher performance and influence.

Let's see how this plays out in a real situation. A client of ours named "Sara" told us that she struggled to keep her emotional control whenever her boss "Bonnie" came near. Bonnie wore a perpetually pained look on her face, and almost everything she said came across as negative, punitive, and corrective. Sara described how her own behaviors changed around Bonnie:

> *I find myself holding my breath when I see [Bonnie], and I try not to move. When Bonnie comes near me, and I'm afraid she's going to talk to me, I stand up a little straighter and tighten my lips together almost like I'm preparing to be hit. And I know I clench my teeth, because my jaw aches if she stays within my eyesight for any length of time. So by the time Bonnie comes right up to me and starts talking, I take a deep breath, lower my eyes, and try my best to give her one-word answers, hoping she'll move to someone else.*

What a wonderfully detailed description, and one that is colossally sad at the same time. Imagine feeling this way at work every day!

Sara possessed great self-awareness about her feelings and behaviors around her boss. Without that level of self-awareness, she would be unable to keep emotional control around Bonnie, much less when facing an MTM involving Bonnie. By adding additional skills, Sara can learn not only to unclench her teeth when Bonnie comes near but also to stay relaxed throughout their interactions.

We will say more about what to do with self-awareness later to improve the outcome of your MTMs.

The ROI of Self-Awareness

It's easy to imagine what could happen if Sara's emotional control eroded around Bonnie. Under stress, Sara could lash out, making it worse. This could lead to lost productivity, visits to HR, and even attrition (of Sara, Bonnie, or even coworkers who got sucked in)—all of which cost a company and culture, money and morale.

Need more return on investment (ROI)? According to research, 75–90 percent of visits to the doctor's office have a stress-related connection (*America's #1 Health Problem* 2017).

Self-awareness provides other forms of ROI, which include the health and productivity benefits of mindfulness, which we will share later.

Portrait of the Self-Aware Leader

Jasmine tried to get a critical project back on its rigid delivery schedule. Not only did the outcome matter to the multibillion-dollar company, but it also mattered to Jasmine's boss Helen who she respected and didn't want to disappoint.

While Jasmine eventually got the project moving forward again, it was still behind schedule. Jasmine's first thought was to send Helen an email or voicemail, but she quickly dismissed that idea. Jasmine realized that Helen deserved to hear bad news immediately and in person, just like Don Corleone in (*The Godfather* 1974) so she pushed aside her own discomfort and went to see Helen later that day.

While Jasmine was talking, Helen never interrupted. Instead, she waited until Jasmine finished before asking follow-up questions. Then Helen spun her chair slightly toward the window overlooking beautiful Lake Michigan. Jasmine thought she heard Helen going "Hmm hmm hmmm." *She's humming,* Jasmine realized!

Finally, Helen looked at her as her tune came to an end.

"Okay," Helen said at last. Then she asked a question, "What did you learn?"

Do you think that Jasmine was eager to deliver this news to Helen? Do you think Helen was happy to receive this news? No and no, right? But this story serves as a short example of applying self-awareness practices.

Jasmine had self-awareness about her discomfort in talking to her boss directly about the problem. That's why she considered sending an email or leaving a voicemail. She understood her feelings (discomfort), but she overrode them to accomplish her higher value: showing respect to her boss.

Helen demonstrated self-awareness of the seriousness of the meeting by offering her full attention, listening without interrupting, and reserving judgment—and even questions—until Jasmine finished speaking. Then, Helen managed any disappointment she may have had before doing something truly remarkable: turning the failure into a teaching moment, a powerful MTM.

How many leaders would have been reading email instead of truly listening? How many would have waited to ask questions on hearing the bad news? How many would have shown anger or frustration when disappointed? And how many would have awareness in the moment to turn a negative situation into a learning opportunity?

Not many. But individuals with self-awareness—who understand their own thoughts, feelings, and actions—can control them to slow down time and navigate MTMs.

Portrait of the Self-Aware Parent

Self-awareness comes in handy in parenting, too. The term "discipline" means "to train." When we give our children feedback about their actions, both positive and negative, aren't we trying to instill self-awareness—so their behaviors are internalized as part of their "self"? And doesn't it stand to reason that by being more self-aware, we can more effectively interact with our loved ones?

We have all either witnessed or experienced first-hand when someone uses passion, urgency, or anger as a justification for reacting impulsively. An all too common example occurs when a parent is addressing a child who is throwing a fit for not getting something she wanted. The parent then demonstratively yells and stomps his feet to let his child know that throwing a fit when you don't get your way is not an okay behavior. The irony of the situation is obvious.

Parents can spend hours trying to train and guide the self-awareness of their children through direct means, but most of what we teach our kids comes informally. Kids learn through our example.

What can you do right now to increase your self-awareness? Here are three strategies to fast-tracking your self-awareness.

Self-Awareness Strategy #1: Engage in Assessments and Learning on Your Personality

Given the connection between self-awareness, building better interpersonal relationships, and generating top performance results, it's not surprising that leading companies regularly administer personality assessments and related training within their career and leadership development programs.

Some of these include Myers Briggs, DiSC, StrengthsFinder, The Achiever, 16PF, Emotional Intelligence, and Workplace Big5. For more information on these, use your preferred internet search engine to learn more and find out how you can take these assessments.

As we've suggested, these assessments aren't always enough to give you a practical "how to." However, they do provide a solid understanding of who you are, what you "bring to the table," what strengths you can further develop, and what deficits you may need to fill to take your skills to the next level. In other words, start with assessments to gain a snapshot of your current level of self-awareness.

If your company does not offer assessments, consider taking them on your own. You can find several free or low-cost versions online.

Where Does My Personality Come from and Can I Change It?

Personality is a complicated subject that could fill a book. To summarize research, you are born with a leaning in your personality, just like you were born with a dominant hand or eye. Added to that, you have experiences throughout your life that affect how you respond—forming your habits. In short, when you combine the best parts of your personality and habits, your strengths surface.

Can you change your personality? Yes, to a degree. You likely will always have a leaning—based on genetics, your history, and other factors. But you can compensate for shortcomings by addressing your habits. You also can analyze your behaviors in relation to any past traumas and let go of habits that don't serve you (e.g., reactions that are based on fear and not reality). Do you remember Jasmine's boss who hummed when she received bad news? It's very likely that she learned along the way that humming kept her from reacting emotionally when disappointed. Changing behavior takes time and intention—and starts with self-awareness that your habits aren't serving you well.

If you aren't sure how to tackle these changes, a trained counselor or coach can be invaluable.

What do assessments have to do with self-awareness? It's important to know your strengths so you can bring out Your Best Self, which we will discuss later. And it's important to know Your Worst Self, for the same reasons. Self-awareness allows you to build on your areas of strength (Best Self) and manage your areas of weakness (Worst Self).

Self-Awareness Strategy #2: Ask for Help Seeing Your Blind Spots

Personality assessments, training courses, and self-analysis are not the only ways you can improve your self-awareness at work. You have nearly limitless opportunities to gain self-awareness each day when you are tuned in to others—especially those with whom you have regular proximity. To paraphrase Yogi Berra, "You can hear a lot just by listening."

Years ago, Ted's boss helped Ted gain some self-awareness about checking his phone during meetings.

Ted told it this way:

> During my performance review, my boss said, "There's one more thing I want to mention. I'm not sure if you're aware of it," he told me. "But frequently during meetings with your team or even just the two of us, you look at your phone constantly. It makes me think you'd rather be someplace else."
>
> Ted was mortified by his boss's observation. When his boss asked if Ted was aware that he looked at his phone throughout meetings, Ted nodded.

"I've always been time-conscious," Ted explained. "I look at my phone to check the time. I'm very careful not to cause meetings to go later than scheduled on my account."

To paraphrase Yogi Berra, Ted heard a lot just by listening. Ted heard that his boss had observed his behavior. Ted also heard that his boss believed the behavior unintentional and provided him with feedback to help Ted "fix" what could be perceived as a problem. Finally, Ted learned that while he might evaluate himself based on his own good intentions, others judged him on his actions alone.

Once Ted gained awareness about his behavior—and how his behavior had been interpreted—Ted changed his behavior. Self-awareness became a tool for change. And notice, Ted gained this self-awareness as a result of real-world feedback instead of a personality assessment (read more on Feedback in the Reflection section).

Johari Window

In 1955, psychologists Joseph Luft and Harrington Ingham created what they called the Johari Window (Johari formed by combining their two first names) as a *self-discovery* exercise (see Figure 2.1).

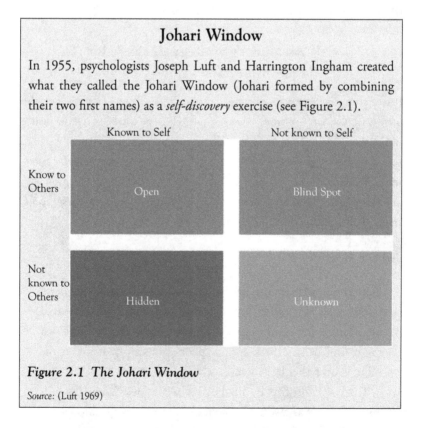

Figure 2.1 The Johari Window

Source: (Luft 1969)

The Johari Window suggests each of us possesses traits that are either *Known* or *Not Known* to us and *Known* or *Not Known* to others. Some traits are known to both us and others, and they are called *Open*. For example, if you speak with a British accent in the United States, you know it, and all those around you know it.

Some traits we alone know (or we think we're alone in knowing) but try to hide because we don't like those characteristics (*Hidden*). It's like a short person wearing lifts in his shoes to disguise his short stature.

Some traits are unknown to us but completely known to others. Those are in the *Blind Spot*. Think of the Michael Scott character on the U.S. version of *The Office*. He thinks he's the best, funniest boss in the world; however, his employees usually see him as immature, selfish, and a waste of time. (If you haven't watched the show, think of anyone who comes across as clueless to social mores and productivity practices!)

Finally, some traits are unknown to us as well as others. Consider these as areas of unlimited yet unknown potential. We might think we know what our lives will be like in twenty years, but we don't. Many things can happen. The decisions we make today influence our future.

If you want to gain greater self-awareness, ask those closest to you about your *Blind Spot*. Ask them what one thing you could *do* or *stop doing* to increase your effectiveness as a boss, coworker, friend, or life partner.

If you don't have someone who volunteers feedback about your blind spots, be proactive. Don't wait until you get called out on your behavior. Find a trusted person you can ask. This might be your peer, boss, friend, or family member. Let this person be a mirror for the things you can't see. You might ask:

- Do I have a "tell" when I'm upset? Bored? Tired?
- What behaviors do you think I need to be more aware of to be a better leader, employee, spouse, and so on?

The Other MTM: Sending Messages That Matter

We are constantly communicating—which simply means we are sending, receiving, and processing information.

In his 1971 book *Silent Messages,* Albert Mehrabian, PhD evaluated the effectiveness of salespeople using potential customers as evaluators. Potential customers found the words used in a sales "pitch" influenced 7 percent of how a speaker's credibility was evaluated. More than words, participants assessed that 93 percent of speaker credibility came from nonverbal communication—vocal tone and body language (Mehrabian 1981). That means whether we want to or not, we often *let our bodies do the talking.*

Most of us have seen this nonverbal communication in the form of eye rolls and glares (especially if we parent a teen!). It also comes in the form of a smile and eye contact.

If you are constantly sending messages, how do you send *messages that matter* (the other MTM)? Sending meaningful, constructive messages starts with having self-awareness, so you can adjust your messages based on intentions—not just emotional reactions.

If you aren't sure of the messages your body is sending, start paying attention. Or better yet, ask others! Because, trust us, they are watching and reading into your actions.

Self-Awareness Strategy #3: Check in on Your Emotional State

Too often, we breeze through our days on autopilot without stopping to give ourselves a "gut check" until something goes awry. Then we become acutely aware of how we feel, which is some form of "Insert Negative Emotion Here _____."

Simply by checking in with yourself, you increase your self-awareness. Two or three times each day, ask yourself these questions:

- What am I feeling at this moment? How am I contributing to this moment (positively or negatively)?
- What's wrong in this moment? What's right in this moment?

You are the subject-matter expert on yourself, so get used to asking yourself regularly how you are doing.

Mindfulness Apps

Of course in the digital age, there's an app for that, should you want some extra help. One example is *Stop, Breathe, & Think*, an app that prompts you to "check in" by selecting a choice of adjectives describing how you feel. Based on your responses, it recommends short exercises to help you clear your head, relax, or check your anxiety. Even if you choose not to engage in their suggested activities, the app helps condition you to monitor your emotions and thoughts to become aware of any drop in your emotional energy. Another popular app is *Headspace*, which provides guided meditation exercises in a variety of topic areas.

Sometimes self-awareness can be lifesaving. But Randy Grimes, retired National Football League (NFL) center for the Tampa Bay Buccaneers for 10 years, knows why some people resist checking in with their emotions.

Randy sharpened his ability to read people on the gridiron, but in his subsequent addiction to pain pills, he became numb.

"I didn't want to face what I was doing to others," states Randy. "I had no self-awareness. I led my family to lose our home—and on moving day, I nearly died of an overdose in front of my wife and children."

Randy finally faced his addiction and found recovery—gaining self-awareness. Today, he is an addiction interventionalist.

"In my interventions, I almost always hear the same thing: denial," Randy told Scott. "'I don't have a problem,' the person will say. People in addiction don't check in with themselves. They deny problems exist. They push the pain away with a bottle of liquor or pills."

To break through, Randy states, "They have to face their emotions fearlessly and learn new ways to cope. Otherwise, they'll stay stuck running to their drug of choice as soon as they feel negative emotions" (Carbonara and Grimes 2020).

How important is it to check in with yourself emotionally? What Randy Grimes says about those suffering from substance-use disorder is just as true for everyone else. Unless we acknowledge our emotional states, our emotions can own us, forcing us to react instead of respond.

In short, when you're serious about developing self-awareness, you'll do three things. First, you'll take assessments to study yourself. Second, you'll be curious to know if you see yourself as others see you. You'll ask others to stand in your Blind Spot and tell you what they see. You'll use that information to adjust. Finally, you will check in with yourself throughout the day, knowing what heightens and diminishes your emotional state. This self-examination allows you to understand your feelings without letting them drive your behavior.

As we stated at the beginning of the chapter, the concept of Self is nonlinear. The many versions of Self are 100 percent you. As a human, you have a limitless ability to turn on or off those parts of yourself, depending on the situation.

And that brings us to the Self that comes out when you try to impress someone. We call it Your Best Self.

CHAPTER 3

Activating Your Best Self

You may have heard the old nursery rhyme by Hendry Wadsworth Longfellow:

There was a girl, who had a little curl, right in the middle of her forehead.

When she was good, she was very good. But when she was bad, she was horrid.

It's a funny rhyme; but isn't it also true? We can be so "good" most of the time. Until we are not.

In this chapter, we will identify how we act when we are at our best—and worst. By understanding your leaning and tendency, you can be more mindful and prepared to manage your Self to Get It Right in your MTMs.

Key Terms: Best Self, Worst Self

Your Best Self is the most positive, productive version of you. Think of the you that shows up when you are well-rested, fed, happy, focused, and firing on all cylinders. This is the you that builds strong relationships, makes the right decisions, and gets things done. People "love" this you.

Your Worst Self is the most negative, destructive version of you. Your Worst Self shows up when you fight with your spouse before leaving for work without food (and possibly coffee!), find yourself stuck in a traffic jam, get a speeding ticket, arrive to work late, and get chewed out by your boss for missing a meeting earlier that morning.

Get to know Your Best Self well, because this is who you want to tap into in your MTMs.

In this chapter, you will learn to recognize the underlying patterns that bring out the best or worst you. You also will gain objectivity about how your day *really* went. Hint: we have many more good moments than bad ones each day, even though the *negativity bias* makes you more likely to remember the bad ones!

Best Self Strategy #1: Identify and Lean into Your Strengths

When you are happy and in the flow of your natural strengths, you enter MTMs with more confidence, contentment, and energy.

In Chapter 2, you learned about assessments to identify your personality, which can be closely tied to your strengths. Now, we will learn how to bring strengths to action.

Flow

Leading researcher in positive psychology, Mihaly Csikszentmihalyi (which rhymes with nothing), developed the concept of *flow*. Csikszentmihalyi believes that people are happiest when they reach a state of *flow* (Csikszentmihalyi 2009). In this state, people become completely absorbed in the task before them to the point that they shut out every internal or external distraction.

If you have ever heard someone say, "You're in the zone!" or "You've found your groove!" you have reached a *flow* state.

Let's try this simple exercise called Your Best Self to identify your strengths in a real setting. Think back to a time when you consistently displayed Your Best Self at work, bringing your A-game, and exceeding expectations, fueled by high levels of motivation. (If you do not have a work example, pick one at home.) Now provide descriptions to the following statements:

Table 3.1 Your Best Self

Describe the tasks and activities you engaged in.	
Describe your confidence and level of competence to achieve the work before you.	
Describe your relationships and level of connection with those around you.	
Describe your level of autonomy in making decisions, planning your work, and accomplishing your own goals.	
What words would (or did) others use to describe you when you were at the top of your game? What words would you use?	

Circle the words that describe Your Best Self in Table 3.1, so you can continually review who you are at your best.

More than likely, the words that came to your mind in the previous exercise included you operating within your strengths. You were in the zone, surrounded by people you enjoy, and engaging in activities that you love.

It is important to know Your Best Self so that you can deliberately do as follows:

1. *Position yourself where Your Best Self naturally shines.* While we are not focusing on the topic of finding the right job role and company in this book, doing so is important to your well-being. If you find that you cannot regularly operate in your strengths within your current role, you may need to re-assess if you are in the right place.

2. *Act like Your Best Self in your MTMs.* This book focuses on what Your Best Self looks like when it is in action so that you can recognize it and recalibrate yourself to align with it before and during your MTMs, tapping into your greatest assets to impact your success. The phrase "fake it until you make it" is a great reminder when you are not feeling it.

3. *Operate within your values.* You have values, which serve as your individual, deeply embedded standards or codes of behavior. When you act outside of your values, you experience shame and guilt, two things that keep you away from Your Best Self. But acting within your values is like an airliner flying with the jet stream. The combined power of jet engines and the jet stream recently propelled a Boeing 787-9 twin jet above 800 mph (Cappucci 2019)! Your Best Self operating within your personal values serves to turbo boost the best parts of you.

Values Exercise

You know your values, but when is the last time you really thought about them? From Table 3.2, circle the five values that you believe currently guide your day-to-day activities. If you do not see the values that fit you best, write your own.

While doing this simple exercise, did you feel tension between *what your values are* and *what you wish your values were* or *what values you are acting on today?* If so, your next assignment is to dig deeper. Make the adjustments needed to realign with the values that fuel Your Best Self.

Table 3.2 Values exercise

Accountability Taking responsibility for both actions and outcomes	**Honesty** Being truthful, sincere
Achievement Aspiring to the highest levels of excellence	**Independence** Free from the influence, guidance, or control of others
Authenticity Acting purely and sincerely within day-to-day work	**Integrity** Words and deeds match, acting and communicating with integrity
Transparency Openly explaining your thinking and actions, since secrets cause mistrust.	**Knowledge** Becoming a subject matter expert who is educated via experience or study
Agility Looking forward to and valuing change, continuous improvement, doing things differently	**Communication** Creating a culture of open, honest, and constructive discourse
Commitment Being bound emotionally or intellectually to a course of action, dedication	**Optimism** Believing every problem has its solution
Competence Possessing the skill, knowledge, and ability to effectively perform	**Improvement** Trying to be better every day
Courage Possessing willingness to take calculated risks and step outside of one's comfort zone	**Passion** Having intense emotional excitement, boundless enthusiasm
Creativity/innovation Leveraging fresh perspectives, breakthrough thinking, and paradigm shifts to create value	**Collaboration** Establishing, sustaining, and fostering internal collaboration and external relationships to build networks

Spirituality/religion	**Family**
Relying on a higher power to guide one's life	Placing priority on spending quality time and promoting health with close relatives
Diversity	**Recognition**
Respecting a variety of cultures/lifestyles	Giving and receiving acknowledgment for achievements
Effectiveness	**Simplicity**
Executing with precision to achieve results	Emphasizing a lack of complexity, complication
Efficiency	**Delivering Results**
Producing results in a timely manner with minimal waste, expense, or unnecessary effort	Holding outcomes as a high aim
Fairness	**Curiosity**
Treating people and being treated equally	Being curious about new ideas, approaches, and solutions
Excellence	**Teamwork**
Striving to exceed others' expectations	Cooperating with a group or team; "together we can achieve more"
Work–life balance	**Friendships**
Being with family, both quality and quantity of time	Fostering relationships and time with loved ones outside of family
Respect	**Fun**
Treating everyone with respect and courtesy	Enjoying life to the fullest
Objectivity	**Volunteerism/service**
Being unbiased and considering multiple viewpoints	Serving the community, non-profit organizations
Environment/ecology	**Wisdom**
Caring for Earth with a mind for sustainability	Having deep understanding, insight, and knowledge, the ability to make good judgments

While doing this simple exercise, did you feel tension between what your values are and what you wish your values were or what values you are acting on today? If so, your next assignment is to dig deeper. Make the adjustments needed to realign with the values that fuel Your Best Self.

Tony: Am I Living by My Most Important Values?

During my early career, I led the learning and development function for a global conservation organization. I was responsible for developing leaders and employees in more than 30 countries. I loved the work, got to meet people from around the globe, and traveled to the most beautiful places on Earth. Not a bad gig.

But things changed when my wife and I had our second child, making for two young boys at home under the age of three. I was also commuting approximately two hours to and from work. A regular part of my role was to travel for weeks at a time. I had a dilemma, because I truly loved my work but wanted to be present for my wife and young children.

My guilt and regret grew about my long days away from home and frequent need to travel. I reflected on my situation and how it aligned with who I aspired to be and my core values. I began writing what values I considered most important. Then I ranked them:

1. Family
2. Service
3. Passion
4. Spirituality
5. Friends
6. Achievement

I realized my current work situation was misaligned with my most important values. I had family listed as my top value, but my daily actions did not reflect that priority. I needed to either accept that at this time in my career, exciting experiences were more important than presence with my family—or I needed to better align my actions to my stated values.

This reflection caused me to look for another role that would balance my need to achieve, serve, and engage in my passions while being present to my family. It took over a year to find, but it did come. To be the husband and father that I desired to be, it was a change that I have never regretted.

ROI *for Best Self*

Gallup Organization has performed decades of research on the importance of strengths as a tie-in to employee engagement. Gallup defines *engaged employees* as those who are "involved in, enthusiastic about, and committed to their work and workplace" (Gallup, Inc 2020). (Does this sound a bit like Best Self?) They found that employee engagement leads to significantly higher levels of performance, retention, safety, and customer satisfaction. A key factor they use to measure engagement levels is, "At work, I have the opportunity to do what I do best every day." Research shows that consistently working in areas of strength improves well-being and performance.

For more on this, see Scott's book *Manager's Guide to Employee Engagement.*

Best Self Strategy #2: Know Your Weaknesses

Now let us do the same exercise called Your Worst Self. Think of a time during your career when you struggled to meet expectations, and you felt burdened by low motivation. Provide descriptions to the statements in Table 3.3.

Table 3.3 Your Worst Self

Describe the tasks and activities you engaged in.	
Describe your confidence and level of competence to achieve the work before you.	
Describe your relationships and level of connection with those around you.	
Describe your level of autonomy in making decisions, planning your work, accomplishing your own goals.	
What words would (or did) others use to describe you when you were at the top of your game? What words would you use?	

Circle the words that describe Your Worst Self in the table so that you can review who you are at your worst.

Which traits do you need to be most aware of, so they do not trip you up? Which do you want to change? How can you use your strengths to compensate for these weaknesses? (We will discuss strategies for keeping Your Worst Self under control in just a bit.)

Strengths Overdone Can Become Weaknesses

Sometimes, strengths can also *become* weaknesses.

Your abilities and preferences overdone or applied in the wrong situations can have a shadow side and become your biggest liabilities. Think about pushing any of the following strengths to an extreme. What traits could develop to trip you up?

- *Strategic thinking.* Taken to an extreme, turns into *analysis paralysis*; more interested in discussion than action; leads to poor execution.
- *Detail oriented.* Taken to an extreme, turns into too much time in the weeds; overly controlling; gets involved in things that could be handled by others.
- *Drive for results.* Taken to an extreme, becomes a bully who steamrolls over people and prevents opportunities for feedback and consideration of other options.
- *Building consensus.* Taken to an extreme, becomes an inability to make quick decisions; decisions result from the lowest common denominator of agreement.
- *Team player.* Taken to an extreme, turns into an inability to say no when helping others; interferes with your own productivity; a pattern of being too friendly at the expense of maintaining professionalism.

All the skills in this list are important or even critical to career success. It is also easy to see how any one of these skills overdone or applied in the wrong situation can become a detriment.

Tony: The Great Debate

I consider myself good at thinking on my feet (a strength I tap into as my Best Self), so I like few things more than a spirited debate. Debate helps me learn, and I like the competitive nature of these interactions—testing my ability to think in real time. This strength has served me well when I need to think on my feet during presentations, deliver training to scientists and highly educated participants, facilitate teams, and address challenges.

Unfortunately, many situations also see this strength become a liability (and part of my Worst Self). In my first managerial role, I got feedback from team members who said I would often ask them for opinions only to immediately play devil's advocate when they were done, or worse yet, while they were still talking. My intention was to learn by challenging one another's perspectives. However, my impact was to make them feel I did not value their perspectives. As a young and insecure manager, I did not understand that my authority and experience in the topics did not lend to a fair debate for my direct reports.

What seems obvious *now* (but did not occur to me then) is that not everyone else gets energized by a debate. In fact, many people shut down, or when they do engage, they feel angry and disrespected. *While none of this was my intention, it was certainly my impact.* I learned how my core personality can misalign with my intentions. I now search for more inclusive ways to engage my employees and build, not debate, their perspectives. While I still share my ideas, I listen more, so others do not feel shut down or alienated by my style.

Best Self Strategy #3: Practice Self-Care

A tipping point that determines whether your Best or Worst Self will make an appearance is also the set of conditions that affect you.

You cannot affect every condition *around* you. But you can influence those *within* you. If conditions around you crumble to chaos, cue Your Best Self to take center stage by caring for yourself.

Entire books and training courses have been dedicated to self-care. In fact, some devote their lives to becoming experts in this field, because there are so many approaches—and it is crucial to well-being.

In this section, we will distill self-care down to five simple concepts to help you bring Your Best Self into every MTM.

Given the dynamic nature of SOAR, as we mentioned, you may need to revisit this list throughout the cycle to ensure you are set up for success. While sailing across the high seas of your MTM, you may need to tap into your greatest strengths as the waves or storms increase. You must be willing to constantly assess and ensure Your Best Self remains front and center.

Five very ordinary circumstances compete with our Best Selves. The acronym HALTS stands for the times when we struggle to be our best— times when we have Hunger, Anger, Loneliness, Tiredness, or Sickness. Developed to help clients in mental health and recovery settings, it is equally applicable to everyday situations. Your Best Self will be most evident if you avoid challenging decisions or difficult conversations when any of these five conditions are present.

Hunger

In the Hebrew Torah (a.k.a. the Pentateuch, in Christian faiths), we read the first example of bad decision-making caused from hunger. After a long day in the field, Esau comes home starving. As fortune would have it, younger brother Jacob has just made a pot of stew. Esau's request for food is met with stiff negotiation from Jacob, who tells Esau that he can have some stew in exchange for Esau's rights as the firstborn.

"Are you kidding me? I'm dying here! What good is my birthright if I'm dead?" Esau responds (our loose, modern-day translation).

For a bowl of soup, Esau exchanges the double-portion of his rightful inheritance.

When you are hungry, your body releases a hormone called ghrelin, which increases your appetite and gastric acid secretion to digest food. Additionally, ghrelin negatively affects decision-making and impulse control. You do not have to be a scientist to know that the Snickers candy bar ad campaign hit the mark when it said, "You're not you when you're hungry." Another way of saying it is, "Your Worst Self comes out when you're hungry!"

Hunger impacts decision-making. A 2011 Israeli university study followed a panel of eight judges who heard prisoner requests for sentence reduction or parole release. The study concluded that while justice may be blind, it gets grumpy when hungry.

Researchers found that judges approved of parole or a reduced sentence two out of three times at the beginning of the day. As the morning continued, judges granted fewer and fewer applications, before eventually granting zero as lunchtime approached! The two-out-of-three approval rate returned after each of the two daily breaks, at which time the judges were provided food. As the day closed, the judges granted almost zero requests (Danziger et al. 2011). While some researchers question the original study, the numbers speak for themselves: hunger impacts decision-making.

Hunger Pains

To let Your Best Self come forward, face your most important work away from a blood sugar drop. Keep high-protein or low-sugar snacks handy so that you do not find yourself at the end of your energy.

Anger

Harvard researcher Jennifer Lerner found that where fear breeds uncertainty, anger instills confidence.

However, Lerner points out, confidence is often misplaced. Angry people become more committed to a plan of action, even when it comes with high risks. Further impairing an angry person's ability to think rationally is that angry people more often seek to punish the individual they see as to blame, instead of seeking a win–win solution (Ma-Kellams and Lerner 2016).

Have you ever felt the need to "put someone in their place" out of what you considered "righteous indignation"? It is called "road rage," not "road problem-solving" when anger—not a desire to resolve the conflict—drives your behavior. Anger will not help you capitalize on important, complex, and relational MTMs. In fact, anger either escalates or chokes the emotions of others near you, pivoting you away from your goals.

Like the grumpiness caused by hunger, anger fuels a desire to punish others. Research with mock juries demonstrated that jurors reported high levels of anger immediately following viewing graphic crime scene photos, increasing their likelihood of pushing to sentence criminals to the full extent of the law (Epstein and Mannes 2016).

Anger drives us to be right instead of maintaining a relationship, to punish instead of diffusing conflict.

In the next phase, Outlook, we will explore factors that lead us to be triggered toward anger—and how to productively manage these emotions.

Tame Your Tiger

Check your feelings and ask: "Is my response to this moment fueled by anger?" Better yet, before going into important conversations, ask yourself if you feel overwhelming anger. Is your fist or jaw clenched? Are you shaking your head in disbelief? Are you thinking about getting even or putting someone in his place? If so, take a step back. Even if you have already entered an MTM when you realize you are driven by anger, call for a time out to pause and collect yourself.

Remember the *Stop, Breathe, & Think* app? Consider evaluating your emotions prior to initiating critical conversations.

Loneliness

According to a 2012 *Harvard Business Review* article, 61 percent of all chief executive officers (CEOs) feel lonely in their roles, a loneliness that hampers good decision-making (Saporito 2014). And, it is not just CEOs; corporate leaders and entrepreneurs in every industry require a confidant to bounce ideas off, give them the latest "word on the street" on how employees are feeling and what customers are saying, and speak the truth when many might prefer to play the role of "suck-up."

Stanford professor and author Robert Sutton warned that loneliness can become a "toxic tandem" of leadership, wherein lonely leaders grow increasingly self-absorbed and less attuned to the perspectives of others when those outside opinions are most needed (Hedges 2012).

One Is the Loneliest Number

Top leaders resist making decisions when the loneliness of leadership keeps them from getting input and support from others. To prevent poor decisions wrought by loneliness, find a peer group where you can talk openly. Consider tapping into a coach or mentor to guide your thinking. Some create a personal advisory board to bounce ideas off of when direct reports or the board of directors are not the best choices for political or business reasons. Tony and Scott go on regular walk-and-talks together to gain an outsider's perspective of the other's life or business.

Tiredness

Bill Clinton once said, "In my long political career, most of the mistakes I made, I made when I was too tired" (Hogan 2019). Think about this from your own experience. If you have ever missed much-needed sleep for a couple of days, did you feel crabby as well as physically and mentally slow? There is a reason for that, and now researchers have found something even more startling: 17–19, hours without sleep impairs your judgment, which is comparable to having a blood alcohol concentration of 0.05–0.1 (0.08 is legally impaired in every state) (Williamson 2000).

When to Say "Not Now"

If you would not meet with your boss, coworker, or employee to address a challenging issue after a few drinks, you should not hold that conversation when sleep deprived. You will say the wrong thing, misread body language, and evade a win–win. Wait until you are well rested. It is usually best to schedule your most critical conversations earlier in the day, before you get fatigued or your blood sugar drops.

Sickness

When you are sick, just like when you are hungry, your brain burns more of its natural food source, glucose. Low glucose levels may cause us to react hastily, instead of thinking about long-term results or ramifications. For that reason, hold off on making big decisions when your prefrontal cortex, the part of your brain that calculates solid decisions, is weakened.

In *Thinking Fast and Slow*, psychologist Daniel Kahneman writes that sickness and other conditions that make us "cognitively busy are more likely to make selfish choices, use sexist language, and make superficial judgments in social situations." Any form of physical depletion impairs our self-control, making us more likely to make stupid decisions (Kahneman 2015). Doesn't that sound like Your Worst Self?

We Are Sick of This...

In some company cultures, taking sick days is viewed as a lack of commitment or sign of weakness, which is hogwash. Those cultures are toxic, both literally and figuratively! The only thing worse than showing up at work sick and making a bad, short-sighted decision is making a bad, short-sighted decision while getting everyone else sick. Look no further than the COVID-19 crisis to see this in action. But even when working from home, delay making important decisions when sickness clouds your judgment. A bad decision today is worse than an okay decision tomorrow when you feel better.

Throughout the day, get better at asking yourself HALTS questions:

- Am I hungry?
- Am I angry?
- Am I lonely?
- Am I tired?
- Am I sick?

If you answer "yes" to any of those questions, be aware that you might not bring Your Best Self forward in that moment. Hold off on tough conversations or difficult decisions until you have solved these controllable conditions.

Scott: A Memorable Velma-ism

My mom was born and reared in Arkansas, where she learned several colloquial sayings and phrases. She directed one to me whenever I went from a delight to a demon because of something unpleasant in my little world:

"It's so easy to be an angel when no one ruffles your wings!"

So true. We can go from our Best to Worst Self instantly when we have not learned the self-awareness and discipline to respond and not react to negative situations.

Were you to stop reading this book now and apply the strategies we have shared, you would be more successful in your work and personal life.

Why?

The truth is, we generate most of our own unhappiness and failure by reacting—usually poorly—in our MTMs when we let our Worst Self emotions reign over our Best Selves. Simply by increasing self-awareness and managing potential HALTS triggers, we can reduce petty arguments and increase your likeability.

Self Summary

We have all heard Aristotle's axiom: "The whole is greater than the sum of its parts." That statement could describe the idea of Self. We are made up of our experiences, environments, thoughts, skills, preferences, personalities, intelligence, physical appearance, and myriad other moving parts. No two people are alike. But all of us can learn more about ourselves in order to practice the skills to bring our Best Selves forward, especially when we face MTMs.

If you have learned nothing more up to this point, we hope we have inspired you to become a student of yourself—to better understand what makes you tick and how you naturally approach situations.

But, of course, we do not want you to stop reading here. While it is obvious that you bring yourself to every encounter in life, you also bring something else: your Outlook. Unless you understand your Outlook, you may struggle to bring Your Best Self forward when you face MTMs.

Remember our sailing examples about heading out on the high seas? That is where you are now, but there are more tools at your disposal, which we will teach you in Outlook.

Self: Self-Assessment and Review

Now that you have finished reading the *Self phase*, read the following statements (Table 3.4) and assess your current proficiency using the following scale:

Table 3.4 Self: Self-assessment and review

5—Strongly agree
4—Agree
3—Neither agree nor disagree
2—Disagree
1—Strongly disagree

1.	I can easily articulate my goals and ambitions.	5	4	3	2	1
2.	I can describe the environment that brings out my Best Self.	5	4	3	2	1
3.	I can describe the environment that brings out my Worst Self.	5	4	3	2	1
4.	I understand my strengths and how to use them to achieve my goals.	5	4	3	2	1
5.	I understand my weaknesses and how they can get in the way of achieving my goals.	5	4	3	2	1
6.	I can name the personal values I believe in the most.	5	4	3	2	1
7.	I consider these personal values when making decisions and taking action.	5	4	3	2	1
8.	I prioritize self-care to address my most basic needs (HALTS)	5	4	3	2	1
9.	I am aware of when my most fundamental HALTS needs are not being met.	5	4	3	2	1
10.	I immediately take action to get unmet HALTS needs addressed.	5	4	3	2	1

Before moving on to the *Outlook phase*, consider making an action plan for any scores that fall lower than a 4 on these statements. Scores of 3 or below represent where you are most vulnerable to *getting it wrong* in your MTMs.

PART II

Outlook

The SOAR cycle—Outlook

CHAPTER 4

Sharpening Your Outlook against Misperceptions

It is not reality that shapes us but the lens through which we view the world that shapes our reality.

—Shawn Achor

Understanding Outlook

We each have an Outlook and worldview. Ours are as unique to us as yours are to you. Your Outlook is based on your natural biases and how you respond to threats. Throughout the Outlook phase, we will share insights about common biases and what happens when you feel threatened. Then, we will outline specific strategies for *choosing your Outlook to succeed with your MTMs.*

Your Outlook is crucial to how you respond in any given situation, because your Outlook determines your action. Think of your Outlook as *your mindset—or the lens through which you perceive and respond to events.* A cloudy, distorted lens creates cloudy, distorted actions; a clean, sharp lens allows you to see things clearly and choose actions that improve your outcomes.

Clearing an Outlook to See Through the Storms

Let us revisit the sailing crew headed to the Bahamas, to illustrate how the skills you learn in Outlook will help you SOAR in your MTMs.

After practicing in the intracoastal waterway, the crew headed out to sea as the sun scraped the horizon. Past the last buoy, they were officially in open waters.

A small squall washed over them, drenching everything on board. The swells grew higher as darkness set in.

Each crew member responded differently, with perceptions ranging from, "We're all going to die!" to "My ship can make it, so let's forge ahead!" to "Our captain must be crazy!" All the skills (gained in Self) were not enough to guide them collectively ahead. Their Outlooks became clouded by their own fears and biases, temporarily paralyzing them dangerously on the open water.

Uncle Paul called upon his previous experiences in safely navigating storms and managing the fears and threats of crew members. He tuned into the radio, crackling on to words, "Small craft advisory."

Uncle Paul then focused on helping the crew regain clarity and equilibrium. "Breathe," he told them. "We'll get there. We just need to stay calm and focus on the task at hand." The crew regained an Outlook that allowed them to choose actions that would get them to the island—eventually. With their threats and biases managed, they collectively turned the boat around for safe harboring in Florida for that night—restarting their journey the next day.

It is difficult to soar to your destination unless you keep your Outlook clear. In the storms of your MTM, an Outlook wherein your perception biases and threats are managed mindfully will guide you beyond the high seas to your intended destination.

Choose Your Best Response

Psychologist and Holocaust survivor Viktor E. Frankl wrote, "Between stimulus and response there is a space. In that space is our power to choose our response. In our response lies our growth and our freedom." Do you know when this truth came to him? When he was held prisoner in a Nazi concentration camp for the "crime" of being born Jewish.

You could rightfully say that when Frankl fomented those words, he seemed to have zero power over his situation. He could not stage an uprising against the armed Nazis. He could not debate his tormenters until they acknowledged the barbarity of their ways and ended their imprisonment of the Jews and others. He could not organize a sit-in until the Nazis changed their ways.

You might suggest he had no reason to manage his Outlook in this situation, because he was helpless. But, is that true? True, he could not control whether he was released or not. But, he could control how he lived in captivity. He could choose to: "Live the best life I can while in captivity."

Frankl further explained his thinking when he wrote: "Everything can be taken from a man but one thing: the last of the human freedoms—to choose one's attitude in any given set of circumstances, to choose one's own way." If Frankl could choose his own attitude when facing slave-labor, starvation, and genocide, surely we can choose also how we respond when we feel slighted, ignored, or disrespected—or when facing our biggest MTMs. In doing so, we master our Outlook and maximize our opportunity for success.

Because MTMs involve many moving parts, you cannot just rely on your self-awareness. You must take it a step further to explore what happens when your Self approaches your most important, complex, and relational situations. These are the points at which you have the most potential—to harm or help; build or destroy; succeed or fail.

Adjusting your Outlook may cause you to adjust course, like a sailing crew might need to do when hitting rough seas. When you adjust your Outlook, your Actions change, enabling you to keep Your Best Self in charge.

What pitfalls must you be aware of to keep Your Worst Self at bay before you enter your MTMs? Read on.

Three Perception Biases that Distort MTMs

You never really understand a person until you consider things from his point of view—until you climb into his skin and walk around in it.

—Atticus Finch to Scout after her first day at school,
To Kill a Mockingbird

Tony: Is What We See Really the Reality?

In my early twenties, I left my new corporate role to work for Outward Bound—an outdoors, experiential, educational nonprofit focused on building skills in compassion, self-reliance, physical fitness, and craftsmanship.

During my first year, I worked with 14- to 17-year-old boys in trouble with the Florida juvenile court system at an outdoor wilderness experience that included canoeing, backpacking, a solo portion, and service projects.

A major component was to help kids work as a community and effectively handle stress. As you can imagine, being away from home, sleeping in tents with the ever-present mosquitoes, gnats, and alligators combined with the Florida heat, did not take long to drive some children into frustration. Conflict was common, either between one or more kids or between instructors and kids, especially during the first part of the expedition.

Instructors would carry a large bucket previously used to ship pickles to fast food restaurants. Once the pickle smell was removed, it could carry paperwork (and hidden treats) to protect them from the elements or even serve as an impromptu chair. Instructors prided in placing "hippie" stickers all over their respective buckets—the more the better.

The pickle bucket was also used regularly in an exercise to help kids work through an escalating conflict. After separating and calming the kids, the instructors would place the conflicting parties on opposite sides of a circle, placing the pickle bucket, decorated on every spot with colorful stickers containing "world changing" or funny messages, in the center.

An instructor would ask one of the kids to describe the bucket. The kid would say it had a large sticker of a flowing river, a smiley face, or a sticker saying, "I heart animals, I don't eat them." The instructor would then ask the other child in the conflict, standing on the opposite side of the circle, to describe the same bucket. He would describe seeing stickers that said, "I Love My Mother Earth," with a picture of the Earth, a multi-colored peace sign that said, "Love One Another," and a rainbow-colored sticker that said, "Celebrate Diversity."

After the second kid shared a vastly different description, the instructor would emphasize how the descriptions were completely different, even though the boys were looking at the same bucket. Then came the important question: which boy's description was right? The kids were encouraged to walk around the circle to see both sides of the pickle bucket. Eventually one of the kids would speak up and say that both descriptions were right.

Finally, the instructor would ask how two completely different descriptions of the same bucket both could be right. The kids would explain that both were correct, because the two kids describing the bucket had different views. The exercise then would move into the teachable moment about why it is important to understand others' views when you are encountering challenging social situations.

Every difference of opinion we encounter comes down to our own points of view. Remembering this makes it easier to view the opinion of another as unique and interesting rather than wrong or stupid.

In your MTMs, you will run into challenges like the one at Outward Bound. A limited, flawed perception of events and situations leads to inaccurate conclusions and eventually ineffective Action. Unfortunately, as humans, this happens to us all the time. Myriad mental and psychological factors cloud our Outlook and stop us from seeing our MTMs accurately. We will explore three of the most common biases that negatively impact how we perceive situations and draw conclusions.

Perception Bias #1: We Think Our View Is Best

Here is where things get a little crazy. Can I trust that others see events similarly to the way I see them? We often assume that we act as video cameras—only capturing the reality that anyone else should readily see. But this is not the case.

It Depends on Where You Sit

Do you remember the research shared earlier about the 220,000,000,000 bits of data bombarding you during the 20,000 moments you experience each day? I think it's fair to say that your data and moments are significantly different than those of the person sitting across from you.

Think about being on an airplane flying by a major mountain. Those on the right side might see it, while those on the left side only see a flat plain—in the same moment.

So, isn't it likely that the moments your mind records are not the same as others'? More disturbing, isn't it possible that both records are flawed?

Innocence Project researchers have helped exonerate hundreds of convicted criminals using DNA testing. Of the 367 people set free by DNA, 69 percent were originally convicted based on eyewitness testimony. Additionally, 32 percent of those wrongfully convicted were misidentified by two or more eyewitnesses! Do you still want to trust your perceptions?

If someone sees a situation differently than you, you might jump to the quick conclusion that he or she is lazy, dishonest, crazy, or stupid. But that assumption fails to acknowledge the role you play in choosing your focus—and the meaning you place on that observation.

Additionally, your own goals, agendas, experiences, values, personalities, and so on, drive your perceptions of people, places, and things.

Added to that, we underestimate that other well-intentioned and intelligent people seeing the same exact situation (and its people, places, and things) can walk away with a completely different set of meanings and realities than our own.

Tony: "Those People"

Early in my career, I worked with a large investment firm. My coworkers were kind, well educated, and what I consider well intentioned. When the topic of the upcoming election came up, it was clear that if one did not prefer the more politically conservative candidate, they must be either ill-informed, uneducated, or blind.

Fast forward four years, I had left the investment firm and was working for a large, nonprofit, conservation organization. Again, the workforce was made up of hard working, kind, well-educated individuals who I would consider just as well-intentioned. In this setting, when conversations came up about the upcoming election, these individuals—with just as much passion and certainty that they were completely right—believed if a person did not prefer the more politically liberal candidate, they must be either greedy, ill-informed, ignorant, or stupid.

Wow, how could this be? Two groups of what I considered smart, well intentioned, and thoughtful people had such opposing views—while very similar access (living near Washington, DC) to information. Their feelings were so different, and I would often hear my colleagues make negative judgments about the character of those on the other side.

We have all experienced bias, when neither holds carte blanche on the truth. This pattern plays with simple topics like two people going to a movie and leaving with entirely different views about its meaning and quality. Some topics are more closely aligned to our core values: like pro-choice or pro-life, gun control, NFL protests over taking a knee during the National Anthem, religion, and so on. You need not look further than your favorite news channel to be continuously reminded of this bias trap in society. The COVID-19 pandemic brought this to light, when politicians early in the outbreak clashed on how to manage the situation—and biases flared about whether the opposite party was making good decisions. And the political chasm only grew deeper and wider around the U.S. presidential election in 2020.

Here are some ways biases play out:

- Our own conclusions seem obviously right to us.
- People can and do reach different conclusions. When they view their own rationale as obvious, they do not feel a need to share why they settled on it.
- People see the differing conclusions as obviously wrong and invent reasons to explain others' rationale.
- When people disagree, they often hurl accusations at each other, making it hard to resolve differences and learn from one another.

It is natural and even healthy that people differ in perspectives, often leading to us to forge new solutions. The trap we fall into is ignoring that well-intentioned, informed, and intelligent people can reach different conclusions about the same situations. This is especially true when others' conclusions differ from ours.

Without appreciating how our perceptions are formed, it is easy to judge unfairly and act divisively. We can be so convinced that our view of reality is an absolute unbiased truth and not recognize how much environment, values, goals, and previous experiences influence perceptions.

Within (and before) any MTM, there may be multiple perspectives in how you view the situation. You may not agree or understand others' *truths*, but awareness of these perspectives reveals a *more accurate* truth.

- Worst-case scenario, you become aware of your differing perspectives.
- Neutral-case scenario, you gain insight into how someone with a differing conclusion drew her conclusions.
- Best-case scenario, you gain more information that solidifies your perspectives or updates your truth to become more accurate.

You will never become an agile or a continuous learner until you expand your thinking from "knowing everything" (meaning holding your own perceptions as absolute truth) to wanting to know more by demonstrating curiosity about others' perceptions. You choose how you approach MTMs. Either you have already made up your mind and other perspectives do not matter, or you value and respect others' views and want to understand them.

- One creates an opportunity to share growth and understanding while increasing trust.
- The other usually ends in debate and argument, with the main objective being to win.

We are not asking you to change your values or beliefs. Quite the opposite, we strongly believe your choices for action should fall within the parameters of your healthy values and beliefs. We are advocating that you remain open to understanding how others have created meaning. Doing so will help your Outlook see more solutions in your MTM.

Back on the boat, the captain seemed oblivious to the high seas, probably because he had experienced them before and could tune them out. But, the crew was sailing for the first time. They perceived a threat. By sharing and listening to one another's perspectives, they decided how to avoid danger. Sometimes, the perception we need most is the one we have yet to hear from others.

Be Agile

Adopt a willingness to respect and understand those with different perspectives.

Let us explore another example of how Outlook can influence our reality.

A couple walked into a realtor office telling the owner Janet, they were considering moving across the state to retire in this town. Before asking about housing options, the man wanted to know more about the people of the town.

"Tell me the truth about the kind of people living in this town. What are they like?" the man asked.

Janet took off her glasses, smiled, and asked a question instead of answering. "What are the people like where you live now?"

"They're a bunch of small-minded, petty, busybodies that do nothing more than gossip!" the man answered, his wife nodding her head in agreement.

"Well," Janet responded, "I think that you'll find the people here are pretty much the same."

The couple left the office disappointed.

A little later, another couple came into the office, telling Janet that they were looking for a retirement home and wanted more information about the town.

"Tell me, what are the people like here?" the woman asked.

Janet removed her glasses, smiled, and asked, "What are the people like where you live now?"

She gushed, "Goodness, it's just the friendliest town. People are warm, accepting, kind, and open. It's just a great place to live." Her partner nodded in agreement.

"Well," Janet responded, "I think that you'll find the people here are pretty much the same."

The couple left the office thrilled, eager to start looking for homes.

Maybe you crave a change of scenery, but what if what you really need is to change your Outlook? If nothing changes, nothing changes. The problem with trying to move away from your challenges is that *you* come with them.

Perception Bias #2: We Do Not Adapt When We Are Wrong

The second major trap in how we view and interpret our MTMs is *confirmation bias*. Once we have established a belief or conclusion, confirmation bias is the reluctance to change that perspective, even if introduced to information that is inconsistent with our initial beliefs. Those with confirmation bias often ignore any opposing information while actively seeking out information to confirm established beliefs.

An Example of Confirmation Bias

David is for increased gun control. In support of his views, he seeks news sources that agree with his beliefs: guns kill people and should be banned. His news sources confirm that our country needs to ban guns. Shelly, on the other hand, supports the Second Amendment, the right to bear arms. In support of her views, she looks for news sources that agree with her beliefs: criminals kill people. Everything she reads confirms her belief that armed citizens, not gun bans, deter crime.

Our own confirmation bias often leads us to seek confirmation for our already held beliefs. Confirmation bias can creep into *every decision we make*—judgments made about others, major purchases, employee performance evaluations, and so on.

How will you interpret your boss's comments on your performance evaluation? If you think she has got it in for you and is looking for an opportunity to fire you, her criticisms will confirm your suspicion. If you expect that she is happy with you and may want to promote you, you might see that critique as a hint about how to tip the scales in your favor. Either way, you are interpreting evidence to suit your expectations.

There are good reasons your mind functions this way, as it serves you well in most situations. You don't have the time or mental energy to constantly check your routine perspectives, and most of the time, it's not necessary. You make thousands of decisions each day, and if you checked your reasoning for every decision, you would never get anything done. Every time you get into your car, you do not want to have to reassess the best way to get to the grocery store. You default to routine thinking, because it is fast and effortless. Add this to the fact that you live in a world where you are regularly fatigued, busy, stressed, distracted, and looking for an easy answer. When you take time to reassess your perspectives, you spend effort from your limited mental energy. As you do not have the time to reason through all decisions, your brain defaults to this approach.

Adding even more fuel to the fire is that the pleasure of being right is one of the most universal human addictions, and most of us spend an extraordinary amount of effort avoiding or concealing wrongness. When we are wrong, we experience incompetence, embarrassment, and humiliation, which are all unpleasant. This makes it really hard to admit we do not have all the right answers and even harder to admit when our established beliefs are wrong. It is easier to rationalize or ignore new evidence than to recognize that we are wrong and need to re-establish a new belief, perspective, or position.

But... this habit does not help us Get It Right when we run into situations that are:

- Important (the outcome matters to your well-being or success)
- Complex (there is no simple solution)
- Relational (it involves at least one other person)

Sound familiar? Let us see how it plays out in a specific MTM.

Suppose your daughter has been down in the dumps since moving to a new school. *The outcome is important.* She proceeds to explain that she did not make the volleyball team last week, no one sat by her at lunch today, and she was not invited to a sleepover this weekend with three other girls in her class. *The situation is complex.* When you ask her what is going on, she tells you, "I don't fit in." You are concerned for her mental health and success. *It's relational.*

However, she neglected to mention that several girls sat down next to her at lunch on Thursday, she got high-fives from her teammates in gym class, and two classmates complimented her outfit today.

The confirmation bias filtered out evidence that contradicted your daughter's belief of: "I don't fit in."

It does not take long to understand how this biased Outlook is not serving her well in acclimating to her new school. If she continues to ignore examples that dismiss her conclusion that she is not *fitting in*, she will miss opportunities to make new friends and engage in fulfilling activities, negatively impacting her overall well-being. This is a self-fulfilling prophecy that could have been avoided.

The worst part is that confirmation bias is not intentional. It just happens!

Research shows the more emotional you are about a situation, the more likely it is that confirmation bias is present. Confirmation bias makes it difficult to update or broaden your perspective, which leads to poor decision-making, missed opportunities, and negative outcomes. Figure 4.1 illustrates an example of confirmation bias at play in the animal kingdom!

Perception Bias #3: We Judge Others Differently than Ourselves

The third major bias that distorts our Outlook about MTMs is *correspondence bias*. Decades of research prove that we often judge another's actions as a result of some faulty personal characteristic, while failing to recognize the situational factors that could drive their behavior (Schneider et al. 2012). When we see others doing something, we assume this is just "how they are"—that is, that they are acting because of their innate character or abilities—and underestimate the influence that external environmental and situational factors have on those behaviors.

In simpler terms, it means when I screw up, my environment was at fault, but when you screw up, it's due to your lack of character, ability,

Figure 4.1 Critical cat

or intelligence. Our most natural, automatic response is to assume that people do what they do based on their personalities and not the situations they face.

A classic example is while driving when someone cuts us off in a merge lane. Our immediate reaction is, "What a jerk!" Rarely do we leave space for a situational explanation for this bad behavior. But the situational reality may be that this person *never* cuts into lines and is doing it this time only because he is about to miss his plane, the one he is taking to be with his great aunt, who is on the verge of death.

Now let us imagine you are the person cutting into a merge lane. You likely grant yourself the grace of letting your situation justify your bad behavior. For example, *I never drive this way; it is just that I am running late for an important meeting,* or *I was about to be late for Johnny's parent–teacher session.*

We forgive our actions and their negative impact, because we understand our situation and believe our actions reflect what a normal person would do. We are less likely to offer the same grace to those who cut in front of us; instead, we assume they are jerks, rude, or bad drivers.

Being aware of your own *correspondence bias* helps to stop you from making inaccurate judgments. It is easy to see how you could assume that someone who does not complete a task on time is either lazy or incompetent. Did you take into consideration that they may have a good reason for not meeting the timeline? Do you know if this person has a history of turning in assignments late? Have you checked with other neutral parties about their experiences with this individual?

Through years of helping leaders provide coaching and feedback, we have found character judgments are rarely accurate or helpful. We have yet to encounter an individual who is *always* rude, impatient, slow, happy, helpful, and so on. There are very few actions that more negatively impact a relationship or kill an MTM than inaccurately or unfairly assessing someone's character.

While many identified cognitive biases affect your Outlook, we focused on the three most common and damaging. What biases trip you up? When do these show up? Be honest. Remind yourself how it feels to be around someone who always thinks their views are correct. Insufferable, right? *Do not be that person.*

With awareness of the biases, when you are wrong—or even if you think you are right—be willing to adapt. Instead of fixating on all the "evidence" that proves you are correct, keep an open mind. Strive to act like an investigative journalist getting the facts from a witness before writing the story. Consider that the story you are telling yourself may warrant a coauthor.

Finally, cut people the same slack that you cut yourself. Your own actions can raise eyebrows at times, but you defend yourself with your good intentions. Do the same for others, instead of judging.

Why is it critical to check your biases at the door before you have an MTM? Because your Outlook will show up in your attitude and Actions. Clean your lens. You will need an unobscured Outlook, especially when you feel threatened. If your perception of the MTM is flawed, then your accompanying Action will be flawed as well.

Speaking of threats, the next chapter will share insights into how we act when presented with a carrot or stick.

CHAPTER 5

Minimizing Threats and Maximizing Rewards

Anyone can hold the helm when the sea is calm.

—Publilius Syrus

Threats to Self

Besides perception biases, other situational elements can quickly cloud an otherwise clear Outlook and sabotage your success.

Most MTMs will instinctively be perceived as threats. After all, you stand to lose something if they do not go well. Mindfulness of the impact of your MTM helps unravel these *threats* and their patterns, so you can diminish their control.

Let us better understand threats and how they challenge your Outlook.

Fight, Flee, or Freeze

Organizations have sprung up to train people what to do in an "active shooter" scenario. These sessions teach us that when confronted with a life or death situation, people respond in one of three ways: fight, flee, or freeze:

- They *fight* violence with violence.
- They *flee* from violence.
- They *freeze* when confronted with violence, becoming a human "deer in the headlights."

Thankfully, you probably do not routinely face threats from an active shooter. But you do encounter threats routinely.

Two main types of threats exist: *physical* and *social*. Let us explore how fight, flee, or freeze can influence your response in each.

Threat #1: Physical—How Do You Respond?

What is your natural tendency? Think about how you would react if an active physical threat walked into your building. Would you charge and tackle the invader? Would you seek shelter? Or would you stand still, trying to blend into the background?

No response is inherently wrong (well, some might be against your organization's policy!). But some will serve you better than others, depending upon the situation.

Wildlife survival experts recommend that your best strategy against a shark attack is to fight back, going for the eyes. Those same experts suggest you remain very still if confronted by a bull, because bulls have bad eyesight. Different animal, different solution.

By knowing your natural tendency, you can increase your survival rate. Your natural response protects you from danger. It is often instantaneous and unplanned. But does it serve you? That depends...

The good news is that unless you are in the military, a game warden, or a first responder, you probably work relatively free of physical threats. At the very least, you will not typically need to use violence or physically run from danger at work. Not only do you not need to react this strongly, but your natural threat response could cause more harm than good—to yourself, others, and likely the outcome of the MTM.

Threat #2: Social—How Do You Respond?

The bad news is that even though you seldom need to physically fight or flee to be safe, your brain still goes on red alert, as if you are experiencing a physical threat.

What could possibly threaten you at work to the point where you are tempted to fight, flee, or freeze? This time, we are not talking about a physical threat; instead, you likely encounter social threats.

Have you ever

- felt like you were losing control of a situation?
- feared you were perceived as incompetent?

- worried that you did not fit in with your peers?
- been troubled that others saw you in a negative light?

If these sound familiar, you have felt threatened. The most common threats from childhood to the grave are *social threats*.

Scott: Bathroom Bullies

The most memorable, scarring social threat of my life took place on my first day of first grade. All of the boys lined up outside the bathroom waiting for an open urinal. When it was my turn, I went in and did exactly what my mother taught me: unbuckled and unzipped my pants, pulled my pants and underpants down to my shoes, and proceeded to relieve myself. My "relief" was short-lived. The class bully, Willy James (of course I still remember his name!), came into the bathroom and immediately yelled out, "Hey! I can see that kid's ass!"

Thanks, Mom, I reflected. *I am the only boy in first grade who does not even know how to pee!* Thanks to the shaming I took on that day, I have since learned a less "I'm-bare-ass-ing" way to do my business. That social threat I experienced nearly 50 years ago forever changed my behavior!

Recently, neuroscience has shown that social and physical threats activate the same centers within the brain. Just like in physical threats, in the face of social threats, your brain processes these threats to help you

- fight (argue or debate your point),
- flight (avoid the person or situation), or
- freeze (disengage from the argument by shutting up).

Additionally, some respond a fourth way: appease (they make nice by simply acquiescing, even if they do not actually agree).

Do you see the potential for harm? If your brain reacts the same way to social threats as life-threatening, you tend to overreact—the emotional equivalent of killing a mosquito with a nuclear warhead.

When Your Reactions Sabotage

The negative emotions, caused by social threats, that show up when you feel threatened can cloud your Outlook and inhibit your ability to accurately:

- Perceive situations
- Solve problems
- Make decisions
- Manage stress
- Collaborate and play nice with others

These are all critical strategies to navigating MTMs.

Worse yet, when you feel threatened and react (or overreact) in your MTMs, you often are not even aware that these reflexive emotions are triggered until it's too late. Your lens, or Outlook, is cloudy. Your emotions become hijacked, and your reactive behaviors are usually counterproductive.

Refer to your situations in Chapter 1 where you did not always Get It Right—or which you are navigating today. Take five minutes to write a couple of these *problems* where you got it wrong, why it went wrong, and what outcome you experienced:

What was your initial reaction? Would your reaction in these MTMs best be categorized as one of fight, flight, or flee?

Table 5.1 MTM outcomes

MTM that went wrong	Why it went wrong	Outcome experienced

Tony's Lone Networking

When I left my vice president (VP) role at a leading research institute to write this book and start my own leadership consulting practice, I experienced new threats and avoidance tactics. Here is one example.

A business acquaintance at a successful consulting firm invited me to a networking event, an ideal chance to build my relationships with local organizations. What could be better? Except, I really did not like networking, and I felt uncomfortable *selling* myself. My entire professional life, I had strived to be appreciated for my *value provided*, versus having to tell others what *value I could or did provide*.

The night before the event, I actively looked for reasons not to go. Full of dread, I even reached back to my friend to remind him that I was no longer in my VP role and double check that he still wanted me there. He did not let me off the hook when he replied that they would still love for me to attend.

In short, my friend handed me an opportunity, but all I could focus on were my fears—like why I may flop or how others may judge me. *I felt threatened.*

My Outlook about my MTM—to avoid the event—could undermine my success in building my network. If left unchecked, these insecurities could seriously handicap my new business.

Have you ever wondered, "What the hell is happening to me? Why am I sabotaging my own success? Why am I having these feelings?" Let's explore.

Your Brain on Threats—and Rewards

Your brain is a powerful, complex tool capable of amazing calculations. Even so, your brain likes to place thoughts into tidy, predefined compartments. Maybe that is why your brain very quickly assesses situations around two primary buckets to help you know what behaviors may be required.

On the simplest level, your mind works tirelessly to

- minimize *threats* and
- maximize *rewards*.

The region in your brain called the amygdala helps you spot threats and take immediate action. When you are looking for a seat in a restaurant, your amygdala steers you away from a table of colicky babies or loud talkers (if you value peace and quiet). It also helps you steer your car away from oncoming traffic before the rational parts of your brain even identify the danger.

Each time you walk into a meeting, your mind almost unconsciously notices all the nuances: who is there, how the participants respond to your greetings, who is sitting next to one another, what is the conversation around the table, what chairs are open, and what kind of donuts are left. Your mind continually assesses all this information and makes a judgment about which are perceived as threats to your interests.

Perhaps a hanger-on from your evolutionary drive to survive, your brain processes threats more quickly than rewards, which serves you well in physical danger. If you have a lion stalking you, you are not likely to decide it's a good time to eat a delicious lunch on a nearby rock as you enjoy the scenery or listen to a voicemail from your peer on a project. Doing so would bring certain death!

Your brain's wiring still reflects the ancient need to survive life and death situations. Because it's hyper alert to threats, it takes longer to process rewards. Being attacked by a wild animal requires an immediate response, but savoring a compliment from your colleague can wait until you get home—or even be dismissed altogether without killing you. Rewards are thereby classified as less important by your brain.

And the memory of rewards fades faster than the memory of threats. You probably remember the time you got in a car accident or had a near-miss better than the time a person let you merge into traffic when you found yourself in the wrong lane. The memory of threat makes you more cautious in similar situations, preserving your survival. It is as if those memories are put in a prominent file where you can easily access them.

Your reactions are also influenced by your past, particularly your early childhood. As your brain and personality developed, you responded to cues in your environment to survive. When you did not get what you needed, you changed your behaviors until you did. Even the most well-intended caregivers cannot succeed 100 percent of the time in providing everything a child needs to feel secure. So, even if you received plenty of reinforcement, you undoubtedly experienced some defining moments that altered your behavior in some way that no longer suits you.

(As we have suggested, a counselor or coach can help you examine your upbringing to recognize patterns that no longer serve you.)

Let us explore how we file past experiences. Reflect on these situations, and then answer the question that follows each:

- Think of a time when someone went out of their way to be *kind to you* in elementary or high school. *How did you feel?*
- Think of a time someone went out of their way to be *unkind to you* in elementary or high school. *How did you feel?*

Which memory took less time to recall? Which memory appeared more vivid in your mind? Which memory had a more lasting impact on you?

Negativity Bias

Research shows the vast majority of people remember times when someone acted in an unkind way but dismiss incidents of kindness. Why? When you feel threatened, your brain goes on red alert, heightening memories for longer and more visual ways. Which is why Scott can still remember the stupid smirk on Willy James's face on that shame-filled day in first grade nearly 50 years later!

While negative experiences are part of life, most of us are not wired to handle those events well. Psychologists Roy Baumeister and Ellen Bratslavsky concluded it takes our brains experiencing five positive events to make up for the psychological effect of just one negative event (Baumeister et al. 2001).

Eventually, your reactions can become habits that cement your Outlook. For example, if you were consistently told you did not sing well, you might eventually merely lip synch until you go silent altogether. While this might not affect your career, how about being told in third grade that you do not speak well in public? If you do not unravel this threat, you could avoid all public speaking opportunities—affecting you well into adulthood and even changing your career course.

What reactions or assumptions no longer serve you?

ARC—Why We Do What We Do

Figure 5.1 shows the three main drivers of human behavior.

We all experience the same foundational drivers for social motivation, and when these drivers are negatively impacted, they also become primary drivers for social threat.

These primary human drivers of behavior are rooted in your most basic social needs. Specifically, according to the ARC model, you need to feel Autonomy, Relatedness, and Competence (ARC) (Ryan and Deci 2000). These are such powerful drivers that you seek their rewards, and when you receive them, Your Best Self flourishes. Conversely, you act strongly to avoid the threat of losing them, and when you do, your reactive Worst Self likely comes out to play.

Knowing your ARC drivers and emotional triggers throughout your MTMs allows you to respond instead of react. Let us explore how ARC can motivate or threaten.

Autonomy

People need to feel ownership and self-direction in their behavior and work.

Think about this in your personal life. If you want to look good in that beach body or avoid chronic health conditions, you may examine your habits around drinking, smoking, weight, daily exercise, diet, flossing,

Humans' Three Basic Needs

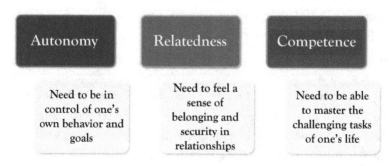

Figure 5.1 ARC model

self-exams, annual check-ups, and sleep more than if your spouse said, "Why don't you put down the ice cream, Tubby, and go run a few miles!?" We accomplish more when self-managed than micromanaged.

Look at the two examples, and ask which would unleash your fullest potential:

- *Example #1:* Though her goals are set and specific, Paula has latitude in how to reach them. She shares her ideas with her supervisor, who supports her pursuit of what she feels is the best approach. Paula works hard to maintain or even grow her boss's trust.
- *Example #2:* Peter has been a sales rep for four years and always reaches his goals. But his new boss continues to look over Peter's shoulder and micromanage his every move. The boss has even listened to Peter's phone calls and gone with him to visit clients. Peter no longer goes out of his way to initiate client contact, because his boss will second-guess him anyway.

Paula has high autonomy, and without the constraints of a micromanaging boss, she will create better results—and feel better while doing them—than Peter who operates under low autonomy and the ever-watchful eye of his overlord.

Relatedness

People need to feel connected to, understood, and valued by others.

Magnetic resonance imaging (MRI) images show that the same region of the brain that records physical pain—the anterior insula and anterior cingulate cortex—also registers emotional pain, specifically feelings of rejection, with the same intensity (Eisenberger 2003).

In simple terms, if you could choose between a broken arm and feeling socially ostracized, choose the broken arm. At least with a broken arm, people will notice, empathize, and hold doors open for you. Feelings of isolation often go unnoticed, intensifying the feeling of rejection and loneliness. Unfortunately, you cannot put a cast on or point to the exact source of emotional pain.

When Emotional Threats Can Cause Real Harm

Researchers at the National Institute of Drug Abuse understand that stress, such as from feeling ostracized, often leads to self-medication ("Are You Self-Medicating and Masking Symptoms of Mental Illness?").

Did you know that the same medication that soothes the pain from a broken bone also soothes pain from a broken heart, rejection, and isolation? That's right. Researchers found that acetaminophen numbed pain regardless if the source was physical or emotional. Not only does that have a huge implication about a leading cause of alcohol or substance abuse and addiction, but it shows the lengths people take to avoid feeling like an outsider.

This phenomenon affects your MTMs, because your pain can drive you (and others) to react in unhealthy ways to avoid perceived threats.

Like before, look at the next two examples. Ask yourself which would unleash your fullest potential:

- *Example #1:* Though Ahmed and his supervisor don't have many shared interests outside of work, Ahmed feels like his supervisor genuinely values him as a person and cares about his career. A few times a week, the supervisor even asks Ahmed for his opinion on business matters.
- *Example #2:* Jody considers herself to be very friendly at work, so it hurts her feelings if people stop talking when she enters the break room. Her coworkers laugh and share inside jokes, but they rarely include her in conversations.

Ahmed feels like he fits in and belongs, which engages him at work. He shares relatedness with his coworkers. Jody feels like an outsider. Her loneliness at work will likely drive her to find another job where she feels like she is part of something special.

Competence

Carrie Steckl, PhD, explains that self-esteem comes from two major aspects: feelings of competence ("I'm good at what I do") and self-worth ("I am a good person and have the right to exist") (Steckl 2020). Believing that we can be effective by applying our talents toward desired outcomes is the cornerstone of self-esteem.

Which of these examples shows a willingness to go the extra mile?

- *Example #1:* Susan managed a mid-sized cross-departmental project to a successful conclusion, using her strong prioritization, organization, and communication skills and receiving positive feedback from all involved.
- *Example #2:* For years, James served as a trainer and subject-matter expert to new employees on using the legacy software system for their enterprise resource planning. Ever since the company upgraded to a new system, James felt behind the learning curve. Not only did his expertise become irrelevant, but he had to go to new employees for help.

The Benefits of Competence

In 2014, *Psychology Today* summarized the business case for working in a role that aligns with areas of strengths and competence with a list of benefits:

1. Increased happiness
2. Reduced stress
3. Increased health and energy
4. Improved life satisfaction
5. Increased confidence
6. Accelerated growth and development
7. Increased creativity and learning agility

8. Enhanced satisfaction and meaning found in work

9. Increased work engagement (McQuaid 2014)

Do you see how crucial Competence is to performance and engagement—and how a lack of Competence can threaten MTMs?

Understanding Your ARC

Which aspect of the ARC model is most important for your motivation, and which is most sensitive to threat? Look at the following examples, and ask yourself which would threaten your Outlook the most:

- *Autonomy.* Without any known reason, your boss starts checking up on your performance and looking over your shoulder. Whereas you once had freedom to decide how to structure your work, your boss begins asking you to explain everything you are doing and why.
- *Relatedness.* Throughout the first 10 years in your current role, you have been considered the hub of office communication. People have looked to you for answers on topics ranging from company protocols to technical matters. However, recently, many new, younger managers have been hired, and you are increasingly out of the loop. Last week, you were notified that your office will be moving to another floor, where not only will you have no line-of-sight with your employees or peers, but you will sit with employees from another division.
- *Competence.* You looked your 50th birthday straight in the eyes without a trace of panic or midlife crisis. But soon after, your career changed direction when your boss asked you to take a lateral move to open a new office. While you have never shied away from challenges, this opportunity comes with strings attached. First, you will be staffing your office with new hires, as you will be able to take only a handful of experienced employees with you. Second, your office will be piloting a new enterprise resource planning platform, one that

you have never used. Finally, once the new office becomes fully operational, you will be given the accounts payable department, which is very different from the billing area you have managed for the last 11 years.

With no awareness about what triggers you, these situations might catch you off guard, and your response might not be Getting It Right.

Now think back to the exercise to assess Your Worst Self in Chapter 3, when your motivation was low and performance may have suffered. Reflect if any or all of your "ARC" was in a "threat" state, in which you wanted to get "away."

- How was your *Autonomy* threatened? Did you feel enough ownership and decision-making authority?
- How was your *Relatedness* threatened? Did you feel like an outsider?
- How was your *Competency* threatened? Did you feel a struggle to perform?
- What were the primary emotions you felt during this time? How did these social threats show up in your motivation and behaviors?
- How did these threats negatively impact your ability to Get It Right in your MTMs?

Now think of your exercise on Best Self. This was a time when you felt motivated, your performance was high, and you were exceeding expectations. Reflect if any or all of your "ARC" was in a "reward" state, in which you wanted to go "toward" the situation.

- How was your *Autonomy* rewarded? Did you experience extra freedom to do things the way you thought best?
- How was your *Relatedness* rewarded? Did you feel connected, like an insider?
- How was your *Competency* rewarded? Did you find yourself in the flow while working?
- What were the primary emotions you felt during this time?

- How did these social "rewards" show up in your motivation and behaviors?
- How did these "rewards" impact your ability to Get It Right in your MTMs?

Situations where it's easy for Your Best Self to shine will create natural opportunities for:

- Autonomy to do your work
- An environment where you feel Relatedness and emotional safety to express your ideas
- Regular opportunities to highlight your Competence

Why Does Your ARC Matter?

The medieval Jewish philosopher Maimonides famously said, "Give a man a fish and you feed him for a day; teach a man to fish and you feed him for a lifetime." Imagine if you fed yourself for a lifetime, except instead of fish, you fed your ARC by being thoughtful about the organizations, roles, career paths, and projects you pursued.

By aligning your role with your ARC needs, you will fortify your Outlook and multiply your satisfaction and productivity.

The ARC Reward

Working on the cultural due diligence part of an upcoming merger, Scott got so focused on his work, he left the office only long enough to shower, change clothes, and nap.

Another team member, Michelle, was excited enough by the work challenge (or crazy enough!) to keep similar hours. One morning, she came into the office at 5:30 a.m. looking...rough. She clearly had not brushed her hair—and had a large coffee stain on her blouse and a small knot on the side of her head.

She responded to Scott's sideways glance by talking about her "commute from hell." She had ordered coffee before boarding the train to Chicago for her hour-long commute. She was so tired that she fell asleep. When the conductor woke her for her ticket, she jumped, spilling coffee everywhere! Having nothing to clean herself with, she drew her legs up onto the bench and fell sound asleep. Her wake-up call at the end of the line was brutal. When the train stopped, she fell onto the floor where she earned the bump on her head.

She ended her story by holding up her hand, looking Scott dead in the eye, and saying, "So I don't want to hear about how I look. I would only show up looking like this to help you."

The truth is, she did not show up for Scott. She showed up because the project fed her ARC. The work fueled her Autonomy, Relatedness, and Competence. And shortly after completing the project, her positive Outlook earned her the first of many promotions.

You are never bulletproof from threatening situations. But when you are aware of a threat to your ARC (or someone else's!), you can *choose* the best Outlook for productive action. Awareness stops you from sitting in the victim seat where your situation and negative emotions batter you. Moving is in your power!

But where do you start? When you feel threatened (and before), how can you use your ARC awareness to slow down and check your emotions, calibrate your Outlook, and choose other behaviors to align with Your Best Self? Let's find out.

Know Yourself under Threat

You have no power to change your actions until you are aware that you feel triggered. What are the signs that your ARC feels threatened? Some of the most universal physical indicators are a clenched jaw, shallow and increased breathing, rapid heart rate, sinking feeling in your stomach, flushed face, and an increase in sweat. (The signs vary by person.)

Think of a time when you felt triggered. *What did your body do to prepare for battle?*

One of the first lessons of self-defense is that you will remain defenseless as long as you are unaware of potential threats. Self-awareness of your most sensitive triggers within the ARC model allows you to consciously choose a response.

How do you teach your mind that not every threat is life-threatening? How can you respond differently in your MTMs? How can you prepare for a successful interaction—instead of a blow-out?

What do you *do* in that space when you feel like blowing up? The next chapter introduces a simple, practical, four-step strategy based on mindfulness to help you clear your Outlook and redirect negative emotions to embolden Your Best Self—When It Matters Most.

CHAPTER 6

Mindfulness in the Moment

Anger and aggression sometimes seem to be protective, because they bring energy to bear on a particular situation, but that energy is blind. It takes a calm mind to be able to consider things from different angles and points of view.

—Dalai Lama

Imagine as a captain, you let the sails on your boat stay in the same position as they started—with no adjustment to storms, ships, or the wind. You may start out soaring, but eventually you would reach disaster.

Managing your emotions allows you freedom to choose your response in your MTMs. If you encounter storms or even a shifting wind, you can recalibrate your course. You can adjust your sails.

The late Steven Covey, who authored one of the most popular self-help books of all time, *7 Habits of Highly Effective People*, wrote, "Look at the word responsibility—'response-ability'—the ability to choose your response. Highly proactive people recognize that responsibility. They do not blame circumstances, conditions, or conditioning for their behavior. Their behavior is a product of their own conscious choice, based on values, rather than a product of their conditions, based on feeling."

Covey said, "You can *choose* the best response for the situation rather than being a slave to impulsive emotions." In the space between stimulus (what happens) and how you respond lies your freedom to choose. Ultimately, this freedom to choose your response defines who we are as human beings (Covey 2004).

Let us go back to a list we shared at the beginning of the book. Ask yourself again, "How would you respond in these situations?"

- You walk in on a work celebration for your newly promoted coworker who took *your* idea to your joint-boss and got promoted for it. *You might want to snub your coworker and his celebration that should be yours! However, you can choose to shake hands with and congratulate your coworker.*

- Your boss presented you a great development opportunity to lead a strategic project completely outside of your area of experience, and you lack the internal relationships to succeed in it. *You might wish to say, "Thanks, but I really like what I do" so that you do not have to fail and look incompetent. Or, you can say, "If you are willing to show me the ropes, I know that I can learn this and be of value."*

- As you enter your home, your spouse starts a conversation showing you that *clearly* you are about to have a heated, all-night argument. *You might rush to say, "And right on schedule, it's time to have this pointless argument yet again!" But you can just as easily say, "I would like to have this conversation, but not on an empty stomach. How about we fix dinner and eat, then talk about this on a walk afterward?"*

- Your most important customer says your organization is not delivering enough, and they are looking for a new vendor. *You might get defensive, telling yourself and everyone on your team that the customer is just a big pain in the butt. Or you could choose to reach out to your customer and ask, "What could I have done differently to satisfy your needs and keep you?"*

- You received a big promotion, and now you are managing your former peers. *You might not recognize the need to do anything differently or even that your former peers might have feelings on your promotion...until they make it obvious that you must do something. Or you could demonstrate empathy after thinking how you would feel in their shoes.*

- Approaching the kitchen, you hear your teenaged son cursing at his mother as he gestures threateningly. *You might raise your arm as if to slap your son while yelling, "Don't ever get up in your mother's face again!" But you could recognize that how you act in that moment of conflict will model more for your son than a thousand lectures.*

- Your new boss has an entirely new strategy for future success, and you do not believe she sees you as part of the solution. *You might feel victimized and start looking for another job. Or you could meet with your new boss, ask her to clarify her vision for the future, and tell her how you might be useful in helping her realize her goals.*

- Your success on a key project is dependent on successful collaboration with a coworker who is not delivering her part. *You might go to your boss and rat out your lazy coworker. Or you could ask your coworker how she thinks the project is going, find out what barriers she might be facing in delivering results, and discuss how to work together to succeed.*

- After being separated from your spouse for six months, your 10-year-old daughter gets called into the principal's office for being sent to school by your ex in a skirt that is too short. While there, you discover that your ex also did not pack her a lunch or send lunch money. Last week, your ex failed to sign a field trip permission slip. Because you are listed first on the school's call list, you are having to deal with this—again. *You could tell the school counselor, "Well, that's just like my ex—never taking responsibility," before hanging up to call and chew out your ex, a conversation wherein you threaten to pursue full custody. Or you could breathe and take time to plan the most important points to discuss to ensure compliance with school rules in the future.*

- You scroll through social media and notice that someone you considered a close friend posted an article with what you consider incorrect information based on political biases. You could block or hide this person online, but you also have to work together on a community project. You stay up all night, scripting responses in your head. *You could type a heated, mean-spirited response to set this person straight. Or you could consider whether an offline conversation to clear the air is needed to pursue your mutual project—or not.*

- As protests erupt around a racially charged shooting, your coworker continues to make comments that make you feel uncomfortable. *You could fire back in spite, or ignore the comments. Or you could gather your thoughts and ask to have a conversation with this person.*
- As a public health crisis emerges, you and your spouse differ in your approaches on how to keep your family safe. *You could call your spouse an idiot and argue why you are correct. Or you could call for a discussion wherein you negotiate a family policy that keeps everyone safe and considers all viewpoints.*
- After months of working long hours on a difficult cross-divisional team project, a manager from another department goes to your boss, asking that you be replaced because "you're difficult to work with." *You might march into that other manager's office asking, "What makes me hard to work with?" Or you could recognize that you and that manager have different perceptions and leave it at that.*
- You wake up on a Saturday morning to the sound of your new neighbor taking a chainsaw to your tree on the property line. *You might run out into the yard waving your arms and screaming. Or you could pause and collect yourself before speaking with your neighbor.*

Let's make this more personal. Think of a recent situation when your emotions turned negative. Remember, most of your negative emotions come from threats to your perceived Autonomy, Relatedness, or Competence. What were you feeling? How did you feel threatened? How did this affect your Outlook—or the lens you were looking through? And one of the most powerful questions is this: What were you afraid of losing?

Every parent who has ever broken up a fight between his kids has heard the children defend themselves by saying, "But *he* started it!" or "I did hit him, but it's because he made me sooo mad!" And, every parent recognizes that those responses are excuses, not reasons.

At this point in the model, we have not shared a best practice or steps to resolve these conflicts; however, we are suggesting that choosing your best Outlook is always your choice. By being aware of what threatens you (your Autonomy, Relatedness, Competence—ARC) and practicing mindfulness (explored in this chapter), you can change your Outlook to respond instead of reacting to the impulse of raw emotions. Let us explore how mindfulness can help you do that.

Mindfulness and Meditation Today

Unless you have been living under a rock, you have heard the words *mindfulness* and *meditation*. They have become buzz words like Zen, nirvana, and a guru doing a deep dive around the horn to leverage synergies and disrupt the peeling of the onion from other corporate ninjas (see why we are not fans of buzz words?).

We like the definition from *Mindful Magazine*: Mindfulness is the basic human ability to be fully present, aware of where we are and what we're doing, and not overly reactive or overwhelmed by what's going on around us (Jaret et al. 2020).

Notice that the definition includes the word "aware" and the phrase "not overly reactive or overwhelmed." What happens when we feel socially threatened? When our ARC is triggered, we become overly reactive or overwhelmed! Under a perceived threat, we react in an emotional, knee-jerk fashion instead of responding in a mindful manner.

But while everyone has heard of these concepts, few know how to act with mindfulness when confronted with MTMs.

Trigger-Happy Hormones

The same stress hormones—dopamine, epinephrine (also known as adrenaline), norepinephrine (noradrenaline), and cortisol—kick in when you are under an existential threat of life or death, or when you feel socially threatened!

Is it any wonder that you might feel jacked up for mortal combat when you get emotionally triggered?

The oldest, most proven way to achieve mindfulness is the practice of *meditation*. When you meditate, you focus on breathing while sitting calmly. Some people meditate to reduce stress or increase focus, while others see it as part of their spiritual practice. *Meditation* can also be used to describe deep thinking, like when you *meditate* on what to say to a friend who is feeling sad.

Scientific interest in mindfulness has exploded recently, with the number of academic papers published on the topic increasing by nearly 300 percent over the past five years. Research has shown how the brain can change in response to training and experience such as meditation (Williams and Kabat-Zinn 2011).

When facing your supercharged MTMs where ARCs may be threatened, mindfulness helps you slow your reactions and choose a better Outlook for success.

Note: This is another example of the dynamic nature of SOAR and how you will revisit concepts like mindfulness from the Outlook phase even in the action phase.

Now be honest: When you think of meditation, do you picture a robed, elderly, bearded monk sitting in the lotus position on a mountaintop while smoke curls from incense wafts about his head? Fortunately, the good news is that you do not have to change religions, wear different clothes, move to the mountains, or feel smoke stinging your eyes to reap some of the benefits of meditation! This chapter will show you how.

Benefits of Meditation

While we explore mindfulness and not meditation specifically, we do want to mention some benefits of meditation. Earlier we mentioned *Headspace* is a great app for learning how to meditate, and they have also written a research paper named "The Science Behind Meditation," which highlights some of the following quantifiable positive outcomes:

1. *Stress and anxiety reduction.* Helps change the way you think about and respond to difficult experiences.
2. *Depression prevention.* Helps you interrupt cycles of ruminative thought that can lead to depression.
3. *Cognitive skills.* Improves your attention, memory, and other everyday skills.
4. *Immune function.* Improves your body's ability to fight infection.
5. *Compassion.* Helps you feel kindness for others and yourself.
6. *Relationships.* Boosts empathy and makes you less judgmental, positively affecting how you relate to others.

7. *Creativity.* Boosts innovative problem-solving.

8. *Pain control.* Helps you relate differently to unpleasant feelings and provides an effective tool in pain management.

9. *Sleep.* Helps you fall asleep quicker and stay asleep for longer.

10. *Heart health.* Has a significant and positive effect on heart health.

Even with all the research highlighting the benefits of meditation, many have not yet taken it up as a regular practice. So, how can either novice or non-meditators reap benefits of being mindful in MTMs? In your moments of triggered emotions and even before they occur, we will show you how to slow yourself down and step into the best Outlook.

Are you starting to see how checking in with your emotions links to the practice of mindfulness?

Three Mindfulness Strategies to Regulate Emotions

Emotional regulation is key to preparing your Outlook to serve your MTMs. The following three strategies will help you achieve emotional regulation when your ARC is threatened.

Mindfulness Strategy #1: Pause

Acting on impulse and raw emotions costs you time, money, success, and relationships. How do you stifle that natural urge to react immediately and instead respond thoughtfully? You become aware of your emotions and pause first. Pausing allows you to catch up with your emotions and not react. Hint: Do this often, especially during the action phase (in your High-Stakes Conversations)!

Two Tales of a Pause (or Lack Thereof)

In the late 1960s, Walter Mischel from Stanford University started conducting tests on instant versus delayed gratification, now referred to as the Stanford marshmallow experiment. In these tests, Mischel offered a young child the choice between one small marshmallow provided immediately or two small marshmallows if they waited 15 minutes. Since the first test, researchers found that the children who delayed gratification to receive two marshmallows instead of one tended to perform better on their SATs, obtained a higher educational level, and maintained a lower body mass index (BMI) (Mischel and Ebbesen 1970).

We wrote earlier about Esau exchanging his birthright to his brother Jacob because he was hungry. It sounds similar to the impulse control test done with children and marshmallows. In Esau's case, his inability to pause, think through his options, and choose wisely cost him his inheritance.

The children who took one marshmallow immediately instead of two in the near future chose to pause to weigh the consequences of that decision. Had Esau been less impulsive and not made a critical decision when he was hungry, he could have practiced the pause, perhaps making himself instead of Jacob (later renamed Israel), the father of a great nation.

We will go into the mechanics of what it means to pause, but first let us explore: *When* should you pause?

Put simply, pause when you feel triggered, based on the factors we have explored. We have spent a lot of time covering what it looks like to get triggered, because self-awareness protects you against your emotional reaction and guides you toward thoughtful response. Being aware of that space is half the battle. When you are on the verge of a reaction, it's hard to pause and think about your best choices. But, when you are aware that you need to and desire to Get It Right, hit your pause button.

Pausing will feel like you are stopping your natural inertia, and you will resist it as unnatural. But continue to review your natural state when you are triggered: your Outlook is clouded, and Your Worst Self comes out! An old Alcoholics Anonymous standby quote is, "If nothing changes, nothing changes."

Granted, it is easier to say *pause* than to practice it under fire. And this is precisely why so many well intentioned, intelligent, highly skilled, and competent individuals make awful decisions in those moments.

Perhaps some simple, homespun wisdom from Mark Twain can help you remember when to pause: "When angry, *count* to four. When *very angry, swear.*" Count to four before you respond. That four-count is your cue to pause. As for the swearing part, go ahead and swear inside your head if you must, but we suggest moving on to Strategy #2 as quickly as possible.

Mindfulness Strategy #2: Breathe

Now that you have paused, what do you do with that space? Breathe. But not just any kind of breath. Breathing is automatic. If you are reading this, you are breathing. We all breathe. Athletes, singers, and public speakers have keen awareness of their breathing, and they understand the link between breathing and optimal performance.

Most of us have an almost intuitive understanding that our breath can regulate our minds and emotions. Have you ever prompted yourself to "take a deep breath" to calm down when things became challenging? Most clinical psychologists and medical doctors use some sort of breathing practice with patients. However, because breathing happens automatically, many do not give breath its deserved attention, nor have we learned to harness its full calming potential.

So how should we breathe to regain control?

Researcher Pierre Phillipot made two profound discoveries about the connection between breathing and emotions.

1. *First, our breathing mimics our emotions.* This one is fairly simple to understand. When you are excited, you breathe quickly and in a shallow manner; when you are calm and relaxed, you draw in slow, deep breaths.

2. *Second, our emotions mimic our breathing.* That means we can change how we feel by using our breath. If you want to get worked up quickly, start taking in fast, shallow breaths; if you want to calm down, take in slow, deep ones (Philippot et al. 2002).

Breathing that Works against You

Scott: The Spider that Stole My Breath

It takes time to change your emotions using thoughts alone. I am afraid of spiders, which I acknowledge is not a rational fear. My dad used to say, "They're more afraid of you than you are of them," which did little to alleviate my fear (however, it did make me wonder how they measure fear levels in spiders). I know the chances of any given spider I see being deadly or harmful to me are in the 0.001 percent of likelihood. Yet my fear persists. Why? It is hard to "talk myself out of" intense fear or anxiety. When I walk through a spider web in my driveway, I do black-belt-level karate moves and spins in midair, all while my wife calmly walks past me saying, "Don't be afraid. It's just a web." Guess what? Her calm, sarcastic comment does *not* take away my fear!

But, Phillipot's research taught me that I could breathe my way through my emotions. How? I tell myself, "Pause. Then breathe. Breathe like I'm calm. Breathe like my wife. When I breathe like a fighting ninja, I flail about like a fighting ninja; when I breathe like I'm calm, I quickly become calm."

This is a work in progress. Check in with me to see how I am doing on overcoming my fear of spiders! Just don't throw one at me.

We take sharp, shallow breaths when scared (whether of something tangible or emotional). That quick intake of air releases adrenaline and other hormones to prepare our brains and muscles to respond to threats—fight, flight, or freeze (in hopes the threat will go away). Additionally, our pupils dilate, heart rate accelerates, and breathing rate picks up to fuel the muscles.

Gasping or taking a sharp breath when scared comes from our autonomic nervous system, the mechanism that primarily controls our fight–flight responses. We do not have to think in order to suck in air when scared. And, the chemicals released in our bodies serve us very well when we find ourselves in a life and death situation—or in certain sports. Picture a boxer at the edge of the ring getting ready for a match, where he or she is jumping up and down, breathing in and out like a bull about to enter a fight, intentionally preparing to react.

But reactions are not so useful when meeting with coworkers or talking with our spouse in an MTM.

Practice Breathing for Emotional Control

Although it is perfectly natural to respond to anxiety with breathing too much, the good news is that we also can change our breathing pattern to promote relaxation. Inna Kahzan, a clinical instructor of psychology at Harvard Medical School, recommends a 4:6 ratio—40 percent of the breath cycle spent on inhalation and 60 percent on exhalation (Khazan 2013). Though the exact breath count that is most helpful for you may vary based on your natural breathing rate (some breathe at a higher or lower rate than others), a rough estimate of this ratio is to inhale for a count of 1…2…3…4 and then exhale for a count of 1…2…3…4…5…6, where each count lasts one second.

While nature has equipped us with a "fight, flight, or flee" emergency response for dealing with threats, it has also provided us with a "calming" response to restore peace and equilibrium, which is essential for successfully navigating challenging and important social interactions. You can trigger a calming response whenever you like by pressing the "button"—your breathing.

Bookmark these pages. As you establish this exercise as a new practice, consider doing these breathing exercises twice each day initially: in the morning and before going to bed. If you have ever tried to teach a puppy how to sit, you know it's not difficult in the right environment: a place that is free from chaos, distraction, loud noises, over-stimulation, and so on. However, once the puppy has mastered this skill, he can practice it even around horses, kids, or other puppies.

Likewise, once you have mastered these five steps, you will be able to expand your practice until you breathe in real time throughout the day whenever you need to gain control over your emotions.

Keep Breathing

You will be able to use the pause and breathe techniques during your High-Stakes Conversations (described soon) to keep your emotions regulated. This is why we are making such a big deal of them!

This is another example of how you dynamically revisit phases of the SOAR cycle throughout your MTM.

Prepare your environment before you begin. Find a quiet place. If you wish, light a candle and play soft instrumental music. Do not put on the television or listen to the news. The same goes for playing music that will tempt you to sing along. As much as possible, remove yourself from anything that will draw your attention away from focusing on your breathing.

Here is our simple readiness checklist:

☐ Sit on the floor.
☐ Cross your legs.
☐ Place your hands on your knees.
☐ Keep your back straight and neck and shoulders relaxed.
☐ Force all the air out of your lungs as you tighten your abdominal muscles.

Now you are ready to practice breathing for emotional control:

1. Take a slow breath in through your nose while counting 1...2...3...4.
2. Hold your breath while counting to 2.
3. Tighten your abdominal muscles while exhaling slowly through your mouth as you count slowly 1...2...3...4...5...6.
4. Count to 3 before taking another breath.
5. Repeat for at least 5 to 10 breaths.

As with any habit, daily practice will strengthen your ability to engage in extended exhalation when in a state of high anxiety, panic, or stress.

Scuba divers master the art of breathing to preserve their oxygen while managing the right buoyancy—hovering above the coral reefs but well below the surface. After much practice, instead of bobbing up and down as they release air from or pump up their buoyancy devices to stay at the right depth, they can subtly adjust location by merely inhaling or exhaling. Eventually, you too will find a subtle rhythm to your breathing that keeps you emotionally steady and maximizes your return on the energy spent.

Five Minutes to Freedom

Each inhale or exhale cycle takes just 15 seconds.

You do not need an advanced degree in mathematics to figure out that 10 full breathing cycles will take you 2½ minutes; five cycles will take you 1¼ minutes. Doing this exercise twice each day at first will take 2½ to 5 minutes. As busy as we all are, we can find that much time each day.

Here is the return you can expect for that 2 ½- to 5-minute daily investment of your time:

- Reduced stress
- Increased blood flow
- Lowered blood pressure
- Stronger abdominal muscles
- Better sleep
- Release of toxins stored in the body
- Increased energy level
- Improved emotional regulation

You have read about how to prepare the environment and engage in the mechanics of deep breathing. To keep this from becoming academic instead of practical, we recommend you read no further until you practice the breathing exercise. Stop and do these steps now. Go ahead. We will still be here when you get back.

How did that feel? What was it like to calm your mind on demand? Did it feel like you had much more control over your own emotions than you realized?

Come back to this exercise often, until it becomes a part of your natural daily routine. And be willing to engage in it even in your High-Stakes Conversations, subtly if necessary (you can take deep breaths as someone else is talking!). This is an essential practice derived from meditation which will serve you in your MTMs.

Mindfulness Strategy #3: Label Your Feelings

Named must your fear be before banish it you can.
—Yoda, powerful Jedi master (George Lucas, Star Wars Trilogy)

Tony: Managing Parental Emotional Triggers

All my children have learned how to push my buttons, but one seems to have become a true expert. He is naturally quick with his words, loves to debate, and has learned if he can trigger me to react, my focus rapidly shifts off the original reason for our conversation.

I always strive to be the best parent and role model possible, but I am not that person when in reactive mode—which usually presents itself as anger or frustration.

After reading research about naming feelings, I decided to give it a try. The next time I engaged with my son and he said something that got me frustrated, I immediately stopped and verbalized to him that I was beginning to feel that emotion. Amazingly, processing and stating my emotion in that moment enabled me to regain my balance, so I could continue in a way that reflected how I wanted to parent. This little tip has been worth its weight in gold in improving my parenting.

Brain imaging now supports the ancient wisdom that psychotherapists, writers, and philosophers have always stated: Simply recognizing and naming an emotion quells its effect, making thoughtful management of future behavior possible. In other words, putting your feelings into words helps you.

According to research led by UCLA professor of psychology, Matthew D. Lieberman:

> Putting feelings into words makes sadness, anger, and pain less intense. According to Lieberman, when you feel angry, you have increased activity in the amygdala, the region of the brain responsible for detecting fear and setting off a series of biological alarms and responses to protect the body from danger. But when we label a negative emotion, Lieberman and researchers found a decreased response in the amygdala and an increased activity in the right ventrolateral prefrontal cortex. This part of the brain is involved with inhibiting behavior and processing emotions.

When you put feelings into words, you are activating this prefrontal region and seeing a reduced response in the amygdala. In the same way, you hit the brake when you are driving when you see a yellow light—when you put feelings into words you seem to be hitting the brakes on your emotional responses. As a result, a person may feel less angry or less sad (Living 2017).

As we learn to identify, label, and express emotions, this area of the brain is strengthened. In turn, we are then better able to respond to our feelings. This is mindfulness in action.

Science repeatedly shows those quickest to recover from distress are those who can identify how they are feeling and put those feelings into words. Brain scans show verbal information immediately diminishes the power of negative emotions, improving well-being, and enhancing decision-making. The simple act of naming your emotion helps your brain move it from the areas equipped to address physical threat to the more rational parts that serve you in problem-solving, relationships, and creativity. At the simplest level, labeling a feeling takes it from an unspecified, terrifying threat to a finite, tangible word, making it easier to set it down and walk away from it. It allows you to mindfully regulate the *volume* of emotion you display to others—which is key when you encounter an MTM with another person who may also have an ARC response! Daniel Siegel says, "Name it to tame it," to show how labeling an emotion diffuses its power (Siegel 2004).

Words matter. It is important for us to develop our feelings vocabulary so we can be as specific as possible when naming our emotions. The more specific we are in naming our emotions the more prepared we will be to take the right steps forward. If you are experiencing a strong emotion, take a moment to label it. But do not stop there: once you have identified it, try to come up with two more words that describe how you are feeling. This exercise helps you uncover the deeper emotion beyond the more obvious one. Table 6.1 is a chart that can help us get beyond the obvious to identify exactly what we are feeling.

Table 6.1 What are you feeling?

ANGER	SAD	AFRAID	CONFUSION	ANXIOUS
Upset	Unhappy	Nervous	Perplexed	Stressed
Mad	Blue	Fearful	Puzzled	Confused
Frustrated	Dejected	Scared	Rattled	Worried
Annoyed	Depressed	Uneasy	Baffled	Nervous
Irritated	Disappointed	Panicky	Bewildered	Apprehensive
Furious	Mournful	Intimidated	Stumped	Insecure
Resentful	Crushed	Insecure	Confounded	Skittish
Livid	Heavy	Shocked	Helpless	Uneasy
Bitter	Lonely	Threatened	Incapable	Cloudy

Know When and How to Let Go

Naming an emotion does not mean letting it own you. Spending too much time on your negative emotions can cause more harm than good. Label them with the intent of defining what you can control moving forward or letting them go so that the negative emotions do not have a negative impact.

Three Approaches to Identifying and Labeling Your Emotions

There are constructive and destructive ways of labeling your emotions. Following are three ways that tend to be safe and make matters better, not worse. Which one you use depends on your preference and the time you have before engaging in the MTM (especially your High-Stakes Conversation, which we will discuss later). Practice all three to determine what works best to clear your Outlook.

1. *Talk to a trusted friend or advisor about how you feel and why.* Feeling heard and validated is extremely effective at sorting out your thoughts and helping you regain perspective to see the situation more positively.
2. *Identify and write down your feelings.* There is power in writing and reflecting. This gets you back to a neutral state and helps you diminish negative emotions and improve decision-making.
3. *Go somewhere where you can say out loud what you are feeling.* This also helps you become aware of your feelings and creates separation between who you are and how you feel. This diffuses your stress and helps you think more clearly and creatively.

Scott: I Am Afraid

When I was a counselor, my client was concerned about her 16-year-old daughter who she believed was on the verge of delinquency.

After listening to her story, I said, "You seem afraid."

She thought a second and replied, "I *am* afraid."

"What are you afraid of?" I asked, because nothing this mom had told me about her daughter seemed inappropriate for her age or dangerous.

"I see her doing things," her mom started and paused for a bit. "I see her doing the same things that I was doing at her age."

"Going to the mall? Going to movies with friends? Having sleepovers at friends' houses?" I asked. "Are these the behaviors that frighten you?"

The woman stared past me for a few moments. She took in a deep, long breath before letting it back out slowly. Then she said quietly, "She's doing the same things that I told my parents I was doing when I got pregnant with her."

Until we identify and verbalize our feelings, they tend to own us.

Let us reinforce the first three strategies for emotional regulation by examining the example of the woman Scott counseled. She went through the steps quite naturally. You can see how the steps flowed into each other.

1. She paused when Scott asked her a question.
2. She thought aloud while trying to "put her finger on" (a.k.a., label) her fear. And then she took a deep breath.
3. She was able to name her fear. She had projected her fear about her daughter's friends and activities based on her own shame, guilt, and experiences that led to her unexpected pregnancy. Once she labeled her fear, she quickly got to its source.

Then she could start learning how to have open, honest conversations with her daughter to prevent another generation from experiencing an unplanned pregnancy. We will discuss how to have these conversations in later chapters dedicated to Action.

If you do not do the three things—pause, breathe, and label your emotions—you will be more likely to react emotionally instead of responding reasonably. Pausing creates a space, stopping action and, more importantly, over-reaction. Breathing floods you with calm, slowing you down to gain control of your emotions. Labeling your emotions prepares you to problem solve, moving away from your amygdala to the part of your brain that can take action. These three steps work in tandem to help you regain emotional balance.

Once you have emotional control, you can choose how to move forward. Hint: your objective is to move toward your best intention and your best goal. Read on to find out what we mean.

CHAPTER 7

Choosing Your Best Outlook for Action

Intention determines outcome.

—Oprah Winfrey

Those who have fought in combat understand the phrase, "the fog of war." In the days of black powder muskets, the ignition of the powder created a blanket of smoke. A shooter wouldn't know if he would hit his intended target until the smoke cleared.

Likewise, when your Outlook is obscured by your biases and threats, you can scarcely see your target, much less hit it each time. Self-awareness and mindfulness help you clear the fog and regain composure when threatened.

With the skills you have already gained, your everyday life will run more smoothly. But without bringing intentionality *and clarity about your goals*, you still may not land on the other side of your MTM with the best outcome.

Back to the sailing analogy, even skills to manage the sail would not magically land a crew at their destination. They would also need to know their destination (goal) and how to get there (intention) to SOAR.

Begin with the End in Mind

"Which road do I take?" (Alice)
"Where do you want to go?" (Cheshire Cat)
"I don't know," Alice answered.
"Then, said the cat, it doesn't matter."
"If you don't know where you are going, any road will get you there."
—*Alice in Wonderland* by Lewis Carroll

This chapter will help you make final calibrations to your Outlook before engaging in Action on your MTM—by defining your goals and intentions.

The Difference between Goals and Intentions

People tend to understand the necessity of setting goals, which is why many books are written on the topic, and almost every performance management or appraisal process has goals as the centerpiece.

But, in our experience, very few distinguish between goals and intentions. This is a lost opportunity, because intentions are critical to your outcome. What is the difference?

- *Goals* focus on a time in the distant future like three months, one year, three years, and so forth. They are your North Star and define the desired destination. They dictate how you invest your time, resources, and energy in your days, weeks, months, and years.
- On the other hand, *intentions* focus on the moment, defining the *what* and *how* you aspire to be in your MTMs. Intentions should align with your best long-term results and relationship goals, but intentions are more immediate and specific to the situation.

Goals versus Intentions

Goals are easy to understand, and each of us has probably set several for ourselves that look something like this:

- Lose 20 pounds by November (for too many of us, this goal remains unchanged…and unreached).
- Finish writing the book by July.
- Plan family vacation to Wales at the end of the year.
- Finish landscaping the backyard before spring.

Intentions are a different animal, because the challenge of meeting your intentions, especially in your MTMs, often bump into your negative emotions. Whereas you strive to obtain your goals

---

> throughout the ups and downs of an extended period of time, intentions can more easily be knocked off course by negative emotions, threat, loss, frustration, or anger. This can allow your intentions to be misaligned with your long-term goals for the MTM.
>
> Your goals and intentions comprise what Matters Most. They include where you are going and how you will act along the way.

The sailing crew had a goal to sail to the Bahamas. But when confronted by bad weather and a nervous crew, how would they intentionally get there?

Intentions focus on how you will act—but they also can include specifics of what you will do to stay aligned to your goal. Take a moment to clarify your best intention before walking into your MTM. Here are some specific intentions you might set along with situations where they might occur:

- Offer unconditional love at my family gathering next week, even toward family members with whom I have had arguments in the past.
- Demonstrate empathy and love to my daughter throughout the conversation about a series of poor choices she has made recently.
- Remain flexible and agile when working with a new coworker on our shared project.
- Provide the best possible parenting to my children, even with a spouse or ex who triggers me or disagrees with many of my approaches.
- Accept the new position I have been offered, try my best to be successful, and intend on learning something new every day along the way.

Think of a goal like a marathon. Slow and steady wins the race (or at least allows you to finish it without burning out). Intentions are like the plan you have for how to run the race—harnessing your focus and energy throughout to keep a solid, steady pace until your relatively short burst of a sprint as you cross the finish line.

The good news about setting both goals and intentions is that you have the power to deliberately carry them into Action.

Relationships versus Results: Choosing Your Best MTM Goal and Intention

It is often tricky to balance both the *relationship* and the *result* aspects of our MTMs. See Figure 7.1, illustrating the balance that often hinges around a fulcrum point.

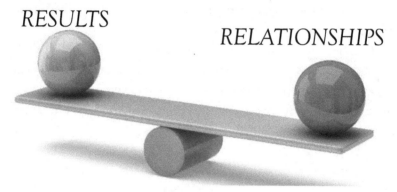

RESULTS

RELATIONSHIPS

Figure 7.1 Balance results and relationships

In his book, *Social: Why Our Brains Are Wired to Connect*, Matthew Lieberman shares that our brains use different networks for handling analytical versus social thinking, making it difficult to be simultaneously good at interacting with people and analyzing data. Even though thinking analytically and socially does not feel different, our brains have different networks for handling these two ways of thinking. These two networks function as a neural seesaw. Lieberman says, "In countless neuroimaging studies, the more one of these networks got more active, the more the other one got quieter" (Lieberman 2015).

Have you ever been deep in task when someone interrupts you with a question, snapping you out of your zone? (If not, the authors invite you to join them any day when they are working from home!) In those moments, you are forced to go from 60 to zero instantly so you can go off on a tangent in a different direction. If you are human, you might get snippy. It is not because you are a bad or impatient person. Rather, it's because you are challenged to balance your *relationship* with the person interrupting you and the *results* you were in the middle of achieving.

In other words, when you focus on the results, it's easy to ignore relational aspects of your MTM; when you focus on the relational, it's easy to ignore the results aspects of your MTM. This is problematic, because your MTMs have both results and relational components that must be met. Remember, MTMs are situations that are:

- Important (the outcome matters to your well-being or success)
- Complex (there is no simple solution)
- Relational (the situation involves at least one other person)

This is why you need to make sure your MTM goals and intentions address the desired outcomes for both the result and relationship. In the case of the sailing crew, they wanted to get to the island safely (result), but they also wanted to have fun, bond, and learn something about sailing (relationship).

Tony: A Van Trip

To understand how this neural seesaw plays out in my life, I think back to when I was trying to get all three of my children into the minivan while running late for some *important* event. After a couple of gentle reminders that did not seem to be effective at conveying my strong desire not to be late, it is amazing how quickly my relational skills were thrown by the wayside. I believe some of the animated threats I have used to get my kids in the minivan have included "grounding them from their phones until they graduate college" or "never being able to play with their friends again." The threat of us being late hijacked my actions, and I abandoned any intention to maintain or grow positive relationships with the people I love most in this world.

Let us practice. Think about an MTM where you need to *do something* in the near future to move it forward (feel free to refer back to the examples you listed in Chapter 1). Now answer the following questions about your MTM:

1. What are your long-term *results and relationship* goals for this situation?

2. Based on the response to the previous question, what are your best "in the moment" intentions for your upcoming interactions to improve or advance this MTM?

Aligning your "in the moment" intentions to your MTM goals allows you to:

- Focus on *who you are* in the most important moments
- Recognize and live your values
- Create a reminder for how you want to live each day
- Live in harmony with your larger purpose in challenging and important times
- See things you may have otherwise missed

By aligning your "in the moment" intentions with your longer-term goals, you bring thoughtful Action. Acknowledging your intentions and goals before your MTM shifts focus off your barriers, perceived limitations, or threats and spotlights what you hope to achieve. Defining your goal and naming your best intention can completely flip how you see an MTM, impacting the Actions you choose.

Scott: Unconditional Positive Regard

My college professor studied under Carl Rogers, a pioneer in psychology best known for the therapeutic concept of *unconditional positive regard*. My professor told me about walking across the University of Chicago campus with Rogers after the completion of a fall semester. A student approached Rogers and told him that he had received an A in the professor's class. Then, the student launched into a tirade about how Rogers' class was an easy A, the principles were overly simplistic, and the concept of unconditional positive regard was an utter crock!

Rogers, according to my professor, offered his hand to the student and said something along the lines of this: "It's so refreshing to hear an honest opinion from a student. Thank you so much for your willingness to be open with me."

Rogers chose to be intentional in that moment, to live according to his beliefs instead of any negative, emotional impulse. Doing so kept Rogers in harmony with his values and at peace with himself.

My professor, witnessing this unfold, told us, "My first reaction was to offer that student a foot instead of a hand," which I dare say most us would have done in a similar situation!

You can live like Rogers, too, by setting your intentions.

Tony: Choosing My Best Outlook

Earlier, I shared an example of being invited to a networking event but feeling sucked in by negative emotions and fears. In social situations that called for me to highlight my expertise, I tended to use humor to self-deprecate or change the focus—behaviors that would not serve me in networking. I realized this was an important challenge in my new business.

First, before saying *no* to the event, I paused. I did not respond out of insecurity by shutting the door that stood cracked open. That fear would prevent me from meeting new people and stepping forward in my next career phase (my goal).

Second, the morning before the event, I focused on my breathing before delving into my feelings. (I was raised in the South, where men were not encouraged to spend a whole lot of time analyzing their feelings, so this was not my natural tendency.) During my quiet time, I deliberately (mindfully) took a slow breath in through my nose and held it for a couple of seconds before exhaling slowly through my mouth. I deliberately breathed through several cycles, then did it again. I could feel myself becoming less anxious.

Third, I identified and named my feelings. I wrote them down, and they spilled out. My feelings (and ARC threats) included:

- *Embarrassment and inferiority. Others may feel I am there to sell them something.* Threat to my Relatedness.
- *Anxiety. Now that I am not a vice president (VP) at a large organization, what value do I bring?* Threat to my Competence and Relatedness.

- *Dread. I don't want to have to sell myself and my experience to strangers.* Threat to my Relatedness and Autonomy.
- *Frustration. I must put myself in these situations to be successful.* Threat to my Autonomy.

Once I identified my ARC threats and labeled my emotions, I gained awareness and control of my emotions. These feelings did not entirely vanish, but they did lose their grip. I could then choose actions to represent my Best Self.

Finally, I named my best intention for this event. I wanted to build relationships and create opportunities for partnership and future work. This was accurate, yet felt entirely overwhelming when meeting new people. It also pressured me to sell and advocate for my value. Focusing on this intention was not helpful, and it triggered more negative emotions.

I tried again to find a best intention that was true but allowed me to engage in this MTM authentically (think of the types of activities that bring out Your Best Self). I came up with another: *My best intention is to learn something and look for ways to help others.* When I shifted away from a *selfish* intention of promoting myself to helping others, my feelings about this event changed. I no longer felt the pressure of selling myself or explaining my value for potential future gain. Instead I could simply try to learn something and listen for ways to help others, even if in a small way.

I am happy to report that I attended, and not one time did I feel like I was acting in a way that was inauthentic or threatening. I learned from the speaker. *Check.* I listened and helped one individual with applying the concepts. I also helped a gentleman by sharing the name of a local person to move something forward. *Check.* I accomplished my intention. I also enjoyed the event!

I left feeling much better about navigating these events authentically. By the way, I did get value from networking, as the host organization reached out for future conversations about partnering.

Naming your best intention helps you, in the storms of life, to stay aligned to Your Best Self, a place where you live your values and rest in satisfaction of focusing on what matters most.

Focusing on your intentions does not mean giving up your goals. By making certain that your intentions and goals are aligned, you can clear your view of the path ahead.

By now, you know enough about your Self and Outlook to move your MTM into Action. Read on to learn how to SOAR.

Outlook: Self-Assessment and Review

Now that you have finished reading the *Outlook phase*, read the following statements and assess your current proficiency using the following scale:

Table 7.1 Outlook: Self-assessment and review

5—Strongly agree
4—Agree
3—Neither agree nor disagree
2—Disagree
1—Strongly disagree

1. I am aware of how my perception biases can distort how I see situations and people.   5 4 3 2 1

2. I actively try to understand diverse worldviews.   5 4 3 2 1

3. I try to understand others' unique situations before making assessments about them.   5 4 3 2 1

4. I am open to changing my conclusions if introduced to information that is inconsistent with my initial beliefs.   5 4 3 2 1

5. I know what triggers my negative emotions.   5 4 3 2 1

6. I am aware when my ARC (Autonomy, Relatedness, Competence) universal needs are threatened.   5 4 3 2 1

7. I recognize how my negative feelings affect my behaviors.   5 4 3 2 1

8. When feeling negative emotions, I always *pause* to gain balance before reacting.   5 4 3 2 1

9. I regularly use my breathing to calm my emotions.   5 4 3 2 1

10. I am aware of my emotions and can accurately describe my feelings.   5 4 3 2 1

11. I stay true to my Best Self when engaging with my MTMs.   5 4 3 2 1

Before moving on to the *Action phase*, consider making an action plan for any scores that fall lower than a 4. Scores at 3 or below represent where you are most vulnerable to *getting it wrong* in your MTMs.

PART III

Action

The SOAR model—Action

CHAPTER 8

Taking Action in Your Moments That Matter

Our results are absolutely connected to our conversations.
—Chalmer Brothers, Language and the Pursuit of Happiness

In the first phase of SOAR, Self, we equipped you to build a strong foundation to engage Your Best Self.

In the next phase, Outlook, we shared how to be on the lookout for the three biases that can skew your perception of MTMs. We equipped you with the skills to understand how MTMs can cause social threats and how to manage your negative emotions through mindfulness. Gaining equilibrium allows you to choose a response (not a reaction) that represents Your Best Self.

But you are not done. You can realize many benefits simply by managing your own emotions and being aware of how your biases can inaccurately distort your MTM. If you apply the lessons from the first two phases, you will gain emotional control of yourself. But, what happens in your MTM, which by definition is important, complex, and involves others (in other words, it does not happen in a vacuum)? Without the right action, your MTM will likely stall. This phase explores those Actions that drive the right results.

Action on the High Seas

After the small craft advisory, the sailing crew left for the Bahamas the next night. That night also brought large swells, as the wind blew hard and the Gulf Stream fought against them. At 3 a.m., under a dim flashlight directed at their course map whipping in the wind, the crew saw trouble ahead. They needed to take Action.

The crew's Outlook was clear and collectively focused on the goal of getting to the island. Instead of being triggered to fearful reactions, they became mindful that they were veering off course. If they left the sails flying, the wind would carry them dangerously far out to sea for a small boat and novice crew. Due to the wind's direction, they engaged in an important High-Stakes Conversation (HCS). They listened to one another's input, and ultimately decided on the shared Action needed: they would bypass the sails and rely on their engine.

They got to work on the solution: fastening the sails down, communicating succinctly throughout. Uncle Paul wrestled the mast while Scott's wife hung her entire body on the steering wheel to fight the current. Everyone knew the goal (to reach the island by daylight) and the *relational* and *task* intentions (to navigate the boat while working as a team).

With the right Self tools (knowing and operating in their strengths), and Outlook (managing their perception biases, staying mindful, and keeping their eye on their intentions and goals)—they took Action together, even amidst rough conditions. They were able to SOAR—and reach the islands the next day in time to catch a fresh fish dinner.

This section will explore Action—how to work together inside your MTM to engage in an HSC and shared steps to reach a goal.

Sometimes Doing Nothing Is the Best Course of Action

David found himself with an MTM involving the performance of a peer on a jointly shared project. As David prepared for his MTM, other matters called for his attention: his daughter broke her arm in soccer, and his boss resigned, leaving the future insecure.

When life interrupts, roll with it. For David, family always came first. As far as his boss resigning, David reminded himself that whatever was going to happen would happen. And, as far as the MTM with his peer, David reminded himself that the issues that created the MTM were not singular. He would see them again, and that is when he would engage—when he was more ready and less distracted.

At times, we all face sudden, emotional MTMs where the best we can do in the moment is to keep our heads: take a pause, control our breathing, label our feelings, remember our best goals and intentions, and close our mouths. While this might look like "inaction" to anyone watching from the outside, your insides know that this requires an enormous amount of thoughtful action.

When the COVID-19 pandemic hit, inaction among millions became the name of the game, as people were ordered to stay home to flatten the curve and save lives. By doing nothing (other than staying home), health-care workers reassured people that they were engaging in the best Action of all.

Do not force the shot. Poorly planned and executed Actions in your MTM can do more harm than good. Pause. Prepare. Be patient. You will be ready next time.

S-O-Action-R

Your MTMs require some Action to advance these situations. What is the primary Action at your disposal? As we previously discussed, your amygdala will only prompt immediate Actions such as fight, flight, or freeze in the social threat of your MTM. Unfortunately, these are not Actions as much as re-Actions to a triggering event, and they are usually not very effective.

After managing your emotions, one Action that most often drives success or failure within your MTMs is how effectively you engage others in conversations. At the heart of any thriving relationship is effective communication.

"Words Create Worlds"

This simple yet powerful quote has been shared by philosophers, theologians, writers, and poets.

Your words are the way you bring to life to your ideas, feelings, thoughts, and hopes. They are the genesis of building communities, companies, causes, and countries. Words have the power to create good and cause harm. Words are the primary way you will build and damage relationships. Something so vital to your success deserves attention. Learning how to use your words within your MTMs is critical to build

> trust, develop relationships, and experience long-term progress toward your most important goals. Your word choice is fundamental to your success, and you need to pay attention to it.

Think about threading a needle. Given good lighting and appropriate corrective lenses, most people can slip a small thread through the tiny eye of a needle. Now imagine threading a needle when you are holding the thread—and another person is holding the needle.

To be successful in "threading the needle" in an MTM, you need to bring forward Your Best Self along with your best Outlook; but you also need to engage in Actions that create trust and mutual respect. The goal of these conversations is not to *win* at the expense of the other's well-being or success. Why? Because the other person is holding the needle! You must work with that person instead of trying to sabotage yourself and the results.

When trying to pass your thread through the eye of the needle held by another person, you need very strong communication, something we call High-Stake Conversations (HSC), which we will address shortly. Those conversations allow you to move your MTM toward the best outcomes.

Too often we think we are having a conversation when we are actually having a monologue. Do you remember when you were a teenager, and your parents had a problem with something you had done? If you do not, you either did not have parents or were much better behaved than the authors of this book! Back in our teen years, when our parents talked with us about a problem like poor grades, breaking curfew, or denting a fender, they did not have conversations with us. They delivered monologues or maybe even diatribes. Our parents often reacted to our behaviors or bad choices out of fear, concern, or frustration. They held all the power. Our role was just to listen, nod, and look contrite. And, more often than not, we would make the same mistake again, to which our parents would respond the same way again.

Monologues do not engage the "listener," nor do they change behaviors. Successful MTMs require engagement, collaboration, and openness between parties. When an MTM gets real, it is time to engage others in an HSC.

Engaging in High-Stakes Conversations

Simple and transactional conversations are easy. You know how to do these, because you engage in these conversations every day when you:

- Assign tasks: "Can you get me bids from three vendors by the 17th?"
- Check on a status update: "Do you still expect to have that report for me by Friday?"
- Give directions: "I'd like you to check with Procurement to obtain a list of pre-approved vendors…"
- Offer a reminder to your teen: "I noticed that you're low on gas. Please remember to fill up the tank before you bring the car back tonight."
- Provide positive feedback around a task: "This is some of your best work. I especially like what you added to the Contracts section…"
- Add your opinion to someone else's ideas: "As I look at your numbers, I'm not sure you used the latest ones. Please check with Betsy in National Accounts to make sure we are working with the same numbers. If you both have the same tally, it's ready to roll."
- Provide helpful information to your significant other: "We are out of the coffee creamer you like. Can you pick some up on the way home?"

After conversations like these, you often forget all about them because they are low-risk and easy. They are memorable only because they are so forgettable!

But do not confuse your everyday casual conversations with HSCs. *HSCs are the action tools you use to address your important, complex, and relational MTMs.* Success with these more difficult conversations requires a unique set of skills and rigor. When you successfully engage in HSCs, both parties should walk away feeling time was well spent. Everyone should feel a deeper, shared understanding of the intentions and perspective of the other. These types of positive interactions create a foundation of trust and set the stage for creating new insights and shared action for progress.

Because of the complexity and threat we feel when encountering MTMs, it's easy to slide into the trap of reactive and defensive conversations. Following are some of the most common conversational pitfalls we encounter in HSCs when we feel threatened and react defensively. Have you ever found yourself reacting in any of these ways in a discussion when you have felt triggered?

- Arguing or debating
- Denying the other person's point of view
- Insisting that you are right
- Citing others as the source of the problem
- Generalizing based on one incident
- Deflecting
- Personalizing
- Shutting down
- Trying to win at all costs

Look at this list and answer: in your HSC, which of these behaviors is your natural default or inclination when you feel your Autonomy, Relatedness, Competence (ARC) are threatened?

Just like you cannot charge your way out of debt, you cannot do the wrong thing and hope that things will change for the better. The right path is one that engages you in a two-way dialogue, providing both parties the emotional safety to "lay their cards on the table" while establishing trust.

You will never reach your full potential, professionally or personally, until you master having HSCs.

Given this fact, it is hard to understand why our schools, universities, and workplaces invest significantly more time and resources developing technical skills and, by comparison, very few resources on developing skills for effective conversations.

A Crash Course in High-Stakes Conversations

In the Action phase, you will learn how to engage others in HSCs that:

- Guard against your built-in perception biases
- Provide greater clarity about how others perceive your MTM
- Demonstrate empathy and build trust with key stakeholders
- Navigate negative emotions and defensiveness
- Clearly state your perspectives and ideas
- Generate insights for shared solutions
- Listen to understand
- Define coordinated action(s)

Think back to an important, complex, and relational MTM when you had an HSC with a boss, colleague, family member, or friend. During this HSC, you felt heard, respected, and understood. You felt that your needs and wants were recognized, and the environment felt safe for sharing and receiving input. You walked away more aligned, understood next steps, and had energy to move forward. In the end, the conversation led to increased trust, clarity, collaboration, and focus for meaningful action.

Now think back to a frustrating, unproductive HSC you have had with a boss, colleague, family member, or friend. There was no real exchange of perspective, and you did not feel heard, leading you to either withdraw or dominate. You walked away more frustrated, with little clarity on meaningful next steps and no energy or desire to move toward a shared goal. In the end, the conversation felt like a waste of time and lessened trust, clarity, collaboration, and focus. Chances are you felt demotivated and angry.

Now reflect on the differences between these two HSCs. How did the successful and unsuccessful conversations differ in how they played out? What can you do to be more effective at engaging others within these HSCs?

Let us explore.

CHAPTER 9

Asking Quality Questions

*I've learned that people will forget what you said, people will forget
what you did, but people will never forget how you made them feel.*
—Maya Angelou

"Before you judge a person, walk a mile in her shoes." This saying acts as
a reminder to practice empathy. But what is at the core of empathy, and
why is it so crucial for your High-Stakes Conversation (HSC)?

Empathy is the ability to understand and share the feelings of another.
Research emphasizes that you must tap into empathy to exhibit emotional
and social intelligence for healthy relationships. It should come as no
surprise that empathy is the cornerstone for effectively engaging in HSCs.

Remember, your MTMs are relational, which means you cannot sail
the high seas alone and expect to SOAR.

Why Empathy? Just Google It

Don't take our word for it that empathy matters—even off the high seas.
Consider a recent research project by one of the world's largest and most
successful organizations. Google wanted to know the secret to building
a more productive team, so the tech giant created a task force to uncover
those productivity must-haves. The project, known as Project Aristotle,
took several years and included interviews with hundreds of employees.
It analyzed data about the people on more than 100 active teams. The task
force looked hard to find a magic formula, but it turned out not to be
that simple. They hit one brick wall after another, as their hypotheses kept
proving wrong. Just because a team was made up of high intelligence quotients (IQs), big achievers, or nice people did not mean they could come
together to produce good results. Even the classic suspects of clear goals,

roles, and team structure proved necessary but insufficient to predict the highest level of success.

They kept digging until they uncovered the one factor that stood out above all others, despite numerous other variations—a culture characterized by *psychological safety*. The strongest teams were not filled with the brightest minds or hardest workers; the number one factor that led to team success was *psychological safety* defined by the following characteristics:

- *People were skilled at reading emotions based on nonverbal cues.* If a team member appeared uneasy with a decision, it was noticed and discussed. If someone appeared down, others showed concern and support. *These conversations are not always easy, but they are important. They allow us to be authentic and engaged.*
- *Each person spent roughly the same amount of time speaking during conversations.* No one ran away with a discussion, and everyone's thoughts were considered. *This practice reflects a shared belief that everyone has something valuable to contribute. And when everyone shares their knowledge and ideas, the group's collective intelligence grows. That leads to better results* (Duhigg 2016).

But I Do Not Work at Google!

You might read how Google creates psychological safety and say to yourself, "Dang. That sounds *nothing* like where I work! When we are in meetings, most people ignore signs of discomfort and tend to steamroll over people's thoughts and ideas that are different from their own."

Remember this: *someone must lead the way*. If you long for this type of culture, you can be the leader who notices when a team member seems to have something to say. You can be the leader who elicits the views of others and strives to create psychological safety. And if you do, those who have felt voiceless and irrelevant will thank you.

Google's data-driven approach highlighted this fact: *the best teams respect one another's emotions and are mindful that all members have something valuable to contribute and should be heard.* These team outcomes are built on the desire to understand the feelings of another.

Google's most effective teams—meaning the ones that consistently outperform others—are made of individuals who actively demonstrate empathy, creating an environment of psychological safety for their members.

Hint: Trust and Empathy Are About Others

In his book, *Trusted Advisor*, David Maister presents research on how a person's self-orientation as perceived by others is the most important factor in either losing or building trust (Maister et al. 2002). Self-orientation refers to your focus when engaging others. Is your primary focus on your needs, or do you also demonstrate actions that show compassion? Research confirms that the single most effective way to increase trust is to demonstrate a desire to understand others' perspectives and needs.

Do those you interact with in your MTMs believe you understand and have their best interests at heart, or do they feel you are leveraging the MTM only for selfish gain? If you are perceived as focused on only your own interests, trust will remain low. To build trust, you must approach your MTM with Action that demonstrates a self-orientation of "we" versus "me."

Neuroscientists have learned that we possess something called "mirror neurons," a type of brain cell that responds the same way whether we perform an action or watch someone else perform that action (Winerman 2005). Do you know the face someone makes when smelling something bad? Just seeing them causes us to mirror their expression as if we were smelling the same foul stench. Similarly, we tend to flinch when we see someone else getting smacked in the face. Talk about a "meeting of the minds!" That is what empathy is: feeling alongside of another.

Empathy, the Equalizer

When Tim Ryan, a recovery activist, author of *From Dope to Hope: A Man in Recovery,* and feature of the A&E special, "Dopeman" talks to someone with addiction, he pulls no punches. But there is a reason why: he empathizes.

"The best recovery counselors aren't those with the best degrees. They are the ones who've lived in addiction. I've lived through hell, so I know what someone with addiction thinks. When I say, 'Addiction will lead you to recovery, prison, or a graveyard,' they know I'm not just blowing smoke. I went to prison, twice. I overdosed and nearly killed a family in the process. Without recovery, I wouldn't be here."

"And I lost my son, Nick, to a heroin overdose," Tim shares. "I'm sick of burying people. I've dedicated my life to helping others, because I know what they feel, and I don't want to sit with another grieving parent if I can help it."

As Tim demonstrates, empathy is not passive. It is a driving force that propels involvement or coming alongside someone to inspire change (Carbonara and Ryan 2020).

In your MTM, you have little control over how others will show up. They may be triggered and reactive, or calm and concise. They may exhibit all these different reactions within one conversation. But *you are 100 percent in control of how you show up.* When you come forward with empathy, you bring a mindset that helps you better understand others' perspectives and become more curious about why they have negative reactions. Generating empathy lays the groundwork for building trust and working together toward innovative solutions for positive change.

Empathy does not stop developing in childhood. We can nurture its growth throughout our lives. This is great news! It means we can evolve. But how? Asking Quality Questions demonstrates empathy and "walking a mile in someone else's shoes" during your HSCs.

Empathy and Quality Questions

The problems we have cannot be solved at the same level of thinking that created them.

—Albert Einstein

You demonstrate empathy when you ask Quality Questions throughout your HSC.

Quality Questions are those that promote thoughtful reflection about the issue at hand.

They can surface underlying assumptions, invite new possibilities, and create a foundation of trust for generating positive change.

Asking Quality Questions throughout your HSC allows you to:

- Stay in learning rather than judgment mode. If you are asking a question, you aren't rushing to provide the answer or solution—or take on the challenge.
- Avoid triggering others by creating a setting where others feel included, autonomous, competent, valued, respected, and safe.
- Improve listening that encourages attentiveness and shared perspectives. To ask is to show interest, and people want to know they matter.
- Heighten understanding of key aspects of people and relationships, reinforcing the idea that everyone is important—and that success involves serving one another.
- Acknowledge the feelings of others to view all sides and prevent defensiveness.
- Uncover the challenges you are facing, creating a clearer view of the situation prior to telling others your perspectives.

For any of this to work, you must bring a willingness to listen and be influenced. You should only ask questions if you are prepared to listen and respond to what is actually being said. Unfortunately, we often ask questions to elicit a specific, predetermined answer, so we feel like we checked off the box of "soliciting input." If you have already made up your mind and will not be swayed on your perspective or decision, then do not ask for input just to get validation or be perceived as inclusive. Asking others for their perspectives just because you think it makes you look like you care about their opinions will drive others to feel deceived, which as stated will create a "me" versus "we" perspective that undermines trust.

Listen to Hear and Adapt, Not Win

Nurse supervisors Anne and Tammy got charged with increasing hospital staff compliance around handwashing after a recent increase in the spread of infectious diseases spread from patient to patient. They decided that Anne would assess the current state by observing nurses on the ward and getting a baseline on compliance. Tammy would assess other possible causes for the spread of infection, like making sure all soap dispensers were full and functioning. Then the two would meet to create an action plan.

Anne: "So, based on what I observed, our current compliance is about 70 percent compared with the World Health Organization's average rate of just less than 40 percent. That means we're better than average, but still terrible."

Tammy: "I'm not surprised. Three of the dispensers don't work, and another four were out of soap when I checked. I think we need a process in place to report, refill, and/or replace broken or empty dispensers."

Anne: "That's a part of it, but do you really think a broken or empty dispenser would stop a nurse from doing what she's supposed to do?"

Tammy: "Well, if it's not easy or convenient, some nurses won't go out of their way."

Anne: "Really? Infections work both ways. If nurses don't care enough to prevent themselves from touching infected surfaces, why would they care if they pass something on to a patient? I don't think that's the answer."

Tammy: "But it's part of the problem."

Anne: "No, I think the answer is peer pressure. We need to teach the compliant nurses to get on those who are sloppy. So, here's what I think we should do..."

No doubt, you have been in meetings similar to this example, where someone asked rhetorical questions often designed to embarrass, shame, or bulldoze the opinion of another. If you have been Tammy, you know how this makes you want to give up and shut up, which is sad. Just as sad is, if you have been Anne, you might even think that you did a great job, and then you would be surprised when you didn't get the results you expected.

Those most skilled at HSCs try to see things from another person's point of view, appreciate conflicting opinions and personalities, and agree to disagree. They manage all this while consistently remaining respectful, regardless of differences of position or authority. But how? They start with Quality Questions, ones that demonstrate empathy and keep the conversation going long enough to generate resolution.

The Art of Higher-Quality Questions

Understanding the "what" and "when" of a quality question is achievable to anyone who wants to improve their HSCs. Choosing *the right type of question* and *when to ask it* can make a critical difference in either opening minds or narrowing possibilities.

What skills are needed to master the art of quality questions? The following are the skills we believe are most critical:

- Focus on understanding rather than judgment
- Start with open-ended questions
- Ask investigative follow-up questions
- Ask paraphrasing closing questions
- Balance asking and telling

Focus on Understanding Rather than Judgment

It is important to understand the difference between a question that focuses on understanding versus one laced with judgment. Questions that contain judgment threaten others' self-esteem. They negatively impact others' Autonomy, Relationships, and Competence (ARC) and can put them in a reactive fight-or-flight state. That is not a great way to create safety for sharing perspectives in an HSC. You cannot stop people from being defensive, but you can control your words, so you don't trigger others' defensiveness. Can you find the judgment in the following questions?

- Why haven't you......?
- Have you thought about......?
- What is the problem here?
- Don't you know better than that?
- Who isn't keeping up?
- Why are you failing at.......?
- Why do you always......?
- How do you keep on dealing with that person or group or situation?
- You wanted to do it all by yourself, didn't you?
- If she is causing trouble, why haven't you......?
- What do you think you should do about this problem person?
- Why is X so much better than Y?
- Don't you agree that.........?

Because of the nature of our thinking, many of our first attempts at questions have judgments built in, either explicit or implicit, which may or may not be shared by the others within our HSC.

To formulate Quality Questions, it is important to become aware of judgments and use them appropriately. So, contrast the question, "What did you do wrong?" with "What have you learned?" The first question assumes error and blame; it is a safe bet that whoever is responding will feel threatened. The second question encourages reflection and is much more likely to stimulate learning and collaboration.

It is often helpful to examine a question for any unconscious beliefs or judgment you may have, because they will impact your HSC. You can do so by simply asking yourself, *"What assumptions or beliefs am I holding that are key to the conversation that I want to have?"* and *"How do these assumptions and judgments impact my long-term goals and in-the-moment intentions?"* Each of these questions invites an exploration into both conscious and unconscious judgment and opens space for new possibilities to reveal themselves.

Start with Open-Ended Questions

Start your HSC with open-ended questions. In the next chapter, we will explore the steps of HSCs and how Quality Questions are used throughout. For now, understand that the benefit of open-ended questions is that they *allow you to find more than you anticipate*; people may share motivations that you didn't expect and mention behaviors and concerns you knew nothing about. When you ask people to explain things, they often reveal surprising assumptions, perspectives, problem-solving strategies, hopes, fears, and much more.

There is a specific anatomy for open-ended questions. See the following:

"Who," "what," "where," "when," "how," or "why" questions lead to thoughtful answers that provide much more information. Because how, what, and why questions are broader, they are better questions than those that jump into the more specific questions of where and when.

Figure 9.1 illustrates the spectrum of these questions.

Closed-Ended Questions   Open-Ended Questions

Yes/no   Which   Who   When   Where   what   How   Why*

Figure 9.1 Closed- and open-ended questions

Yes/No Versus Why?

A favorite tool used by lawyers in the courtroom is the Yes/No question. The reason they like these questions is the same reason these questions fail when trying to gain perspective: Yes/No shuts out the possibility of hearing unwanted explanations, points of view, or details. Yes/No questions, by design, lead a person to answering down a very narrow corridor, one stripped of nuance or perspective.

The authors admit that while they don't practice law in the courtroom, they sometimes use the same approach as parents of teens:

Dad: "Did you take my car without asking?"

Teenager: "Yes, but…"

Dad: "Just Yes or No. And did you think I wouldn't find out?"

Teenager: "Well, I…"

Dad: "Just Yes or No."

Teenager: "Well, I didn't think about it."

Dad: "That's the problem. You don't think. Isn't that right?"

It is hard to imagine this line of questioning leading to a warm embrace, right? While Yes/No questions get to a version of the facts, they miss most of them. For example, what if the teen's mom gave permission for the teen to go to the pharmacy to pick up a prescription? Yes/No questions don't allow for critical details to surface.

On the other end of the spectrum, *why* questions are important for understanding one's purpose and intentions, especially when they come from a place of genuine curiosity and interest like, "I wonder why that happened?"

Just be careful with frequently asking questions that begin with "Why." Asking a series of why questions without fully established trust can leave a person feeling defensive, as if you expect that person to justify her actions.

By using words on the right side of the continuum in Figure 9.1, we can make many of our questions more open-ended. For example, consider the following sequence:

- Are you satisfied with our relationship?
- When have you been most satisfied with our relationship?
- What is it about our relationship that you find most satisfying?
- Why do you think our relationship has had ups and downs?

Open-ended Quality Questions provoke thoughtful exploration and creative thinking. Start your HSCs with broader scope questions to encourage new ideas and possibilities.

Ask Follow-Up Questions and Listen

After starting with open-ended Quality Questions in your HSC, investigate deeper by asking follow-up questions. This skill shines a light on others' best thinking and insights. Follow-up questions hold special power. They signal that you are listening, care, and want to know more. People interacting with someone who asks lots of follow-up questions feel respected and heard. An unexpected benefit of follow-up questions is that they do not require much preparation, because they come about naturally if your true intention is to create deeper understanding.

Intellectual Curiosity

Stephen Mueller served in the Middle East with the U.S. Marine Corps. When he and his fellow Marines had downtime, they visited historic sites. On one occasion, they ventured into the city of Petra in southern Jordan. As soon as they arrived in the historic city, most of the Marines went inside the numerous tourist traps to look for souvenirs and trinkets. When they finished, they noticed that Stephen was not with them. His fellow Marines searched for him in all the shops before breaking into smaller squads to find him.

A few minutes later, one squad entered a tent at the fringe of the city. Inside the tent, they found Stephen on the ground drinking tea with his host. The two of them were discussing *Bedouin* history and local legends.

Stephen later said, "My favorite part of traveling the Middle East was to sit with the locals and learn from them. I could listen to them for hours" (Carbonara and Mueller 2019).

People with intellectual curiosity ask better questions—Quality Questions—and get more relevant, meaningful answers.

The art of asking great follow-up questions lies in your ability to *allow for silence*. Follow-up questions dig deeper into another's thinking by asking an additional question such as "What else do you think about the situation?" "What makes you say that?" "Would you say more about that?" or "Could you give me an example?" Get comfortable with asking an open-ended quality question, waiting for and listening to a response, and then waiting some more for the dam to break. If you resist the need to fill the gaps in the conversation, often the other person will reveal more meaningful information.

Too often, our insecurity with silence rushes us to fill in the gap, which never allows your conversation partner to construct his entire response. Impatience causes both you and your conversation partner to miss the good stuff. Allowing others to think more deeply about what you are asking helps them articulate the thinking behind their perspective and intent. Using basic *tell me more* questions helps people go deeper. Here are some examples:

- Can you tell me more about that...?
- What exactly does that mean for you?
- How does this relate to what we have been talking about?
- What do we already know about this?
- How does that impact you achieving your desired outcome?
- Can you give me an example?
- Can you rephrase that, please, so I can be sure that I understand what you mean?

Paraphrase and Ask Closed-Ended Questions

Closed-ended questions hold limited response options. Typically, they begin with "would," "should," "is," "are," and "do you think," which lead to "yes" or "no" answers.

Closed-ended questions, when misused, can shut down conversation, but they still have a place within your HSC. They can be strategically used to ensure you and your HSC partner align in shared understanding about what was said and what it means.

Closed-ended question should almost always be paired with paraphrasing, which is stating back, in your own words, what you understood the other person has said. Effective paraphrasing clarifies misunderstanding before moving on to another topic.

Start paraphrasing from the "I" perspective, so your conversation partner knows that you own your perception of what they said. Your perception might be different than what the speaker said or intended to say. Paraphrasing usually begins with the following types of phrases:

- So what I hear you saying is…
- What I understand you to say is…
- If I understand you correctly, you are saying…
- Are you saying … or …?
- Let me make sure I'm following, you are saying…?
- You seem to feel strongly that…

Effective paraphrasing is followed by a closed-ended question to ensure agreement and check that your assumptions are correct. An example is, "So what I hear you saying is that you are frustrated by the lack of response from my team when you have made a complaint about xyz. Is that correct?" (Note the open-ended Yes/No question at the end.) This practice shows transparency, which builds trust and allows for adjustment of your assumptions if incorrect.

Balance Asking and Telling

A conversation is a flow that requires participants to be in sync; it's a rhythmic dance that unfolds over time. Just as Quality Questions can increase trust, the way you tell your perspectives is part of collaboration. No one wants to be the only one sharing in a conversation. It feels one-sided, like an inquisition. Putting someone on the defensive erodes trust. Remember your HSC should reflect joint willingness to share perspectives, intentions, assumptions, and ongoing solutions.

As stated earlier, asking questions demonstrates your willingness to listen, but that does not minimize your role in sharing, as this creates transparency with your HSC partner.

Aim to create an inclusive conversation where everyone has input and influence. Each step of your HSC should appropriately balance asking and telling from each participant, fostering psychological safety and solutions.

Keep in mind that this is *your* MTM. Stating your perspectives, intentions, and solutions about the MTM requires that you state the facts you know, express your feelings, and share your ideas for action. Here are some quick tips for telling your perspectives during your HSC:

- State your assumptions and describe the data that led to your conclusions.
- Use "I statements." (*I feel, I believe, I thought, etc.*) Do not speak for others. (*We feel, everyone believes, they thought, etc.*)
- Give specific examples of what you propose, even if hypothetical or metaphorical.
- Respond by using "Yes," and statements instead of "Yes," but, to add to others' perspectives and increase buy-in.
- Encourage others to share their perspectives about your assumptions.
- Avoid showing defensiveness when your ideas are questioned.
- Even when advocating your own position, stay open and listen; this will encourage others to listen to your point of view and share more candidly.

Scott: Get Good at the Volley

I grew up playing table tennis. When I had no one else to play with, I would beg my sister, Donna, to pick up a paddle. But because I played more than she did, I had more skill. I couldn't blame her for not wanting to play me when the outcome seemed predetermined.

By accident, I stumbled on a way to get her to play while also helping her improve. I suggested that we see how long we could keep a volley going. At first, I had to slow down my hits so she could return the ball. But as our volleys grew in lengths to hundreds of back-and-forths, we found a natural rhythm, and she got better. Heck, I got better! We ended up with more than 700 consecutive returns!

Getting good at creating and asking Quality Questions doesn't mean you come prepared to an HSC with a list of questions looking for answers, and that you sit quietly, simply asking and listening, until you have finished your list.

The process is reciprocal, like me keeping a volley going with my sister; regardless of who serves the ball, it was a back-and-forth exchange where the goal was to return the volley.

Use Quality Questions to help open your conversation, set the tone, and gain the other's perspective.

Growth Mindset and Quality Questions

When you master the art of asking Quality Questions, a main benefit is that you foster a growth mindset.

Carol Dweck suggests in *Mindset* that we can operate in either a fixed or growth mindset. Dweck's research says people can be split into two categories: those with a "fixed mindset" believe their capabilities are already set, while those with a "growth mindset" believe they can enhance their basic qualities through effort. People who hold a growth mindset believe theirs and others' intelligence can be developed, that the brain is like a muscle that can be trained. This feeds the desire to learn, grow, and improve (Dweck 2017).

When engaging others in your MTM, bring a growth mindset, believing that you can influence, grow, and impact others.

We all fluctuate between having a growth and fixed mindset. For example, you may have a fixed mindset that you are a terrible singer. You then believe it a waste of time to improve your singing, which is okay, if singing poorly doesn't affect your goals. But, what if you had a fixed mindset that you couldn't have a good relationship with one of your children, or your wife or boss? In turn, that would lead to a belief that putting additional effort to improve the relationship would be foolish, as you think this bad relationship will never change.

Whew—wait a minute. Having a good relationship with these loved ones or boss likely really matters to you and your core personal goals. You can shift toward a growth mindset—believing your effort matters and your relationship can be improved. Strive to focus on new ways to engage, understand, and compromise. See how this works?

Quality Questions allow relationships to evolve. It's hard to keep a fixed mindset when you truly want to learn more about others' perspectives and generate ideas for future success!

Now that you have the components of Quality Questions, let's put them into action in your HSCs!

CHAPTER 10

Four Steps for Successful High-Stakes Conversations

Leadership is a way of thinking, a way of acting, and, most importantly, a way of communicating.

—Simon Sinek

Up to this point, we have laid out everything you need to get started. We have charted your course. Now it is time to build the Action of conducting an effective High-Stakes Conversation (HSC).

You've practiced your pause, reviewed your breathing strategy to stay on top of your own negative emotions, and evaluated your own ARC (Autonomy, Relationships, Competence) and biases. You've been deliberate about ensuring your "in-the-moment intentions" are aligned to your longer-term goals. You've considered how open-ended questions can demonstrate collaboration and empathy. You've also thought through the type of questions and statements that generate or rebuild trust.

Now what?

The following section outlines the Four Steps of Conducting HSCs. No conversation is predictable or linear, but understanding the framework and a general flow for successful HSCs will help you put your thoughts and Actions together in your MTM.

High-Stakes Conversation Step #1: Align on the Issue

Defining and getting consensus on the issue is central to your HSC. If you fail to reach consensus about the challenge, a successful conversation will elude you, because each person will be solving different issues.

Don't assume that you both share the same definition, root cause, or ideas about the problem. You might not even agree that you have a problem, so you cannot possibly start discussing obstacles or solutions!

Positive Issues

An issue is not always negative. It can just as often be about a new venture, idea, or opportunity.

To start your HSC, you must introduce the MTM you want to discuss. The goal is to quickly provide your perception of the issue you would like to discuss and answer any clarifying questions. Following are some examples about how to introduce the issue.

- I would like to talk about _____ with you so that we can move forward, but first I would like to get your point of view.
- I need your help with what just happened. Do you have a few minutes to talk?
- I think we have different perceptions about _____. I would like to hear your thoughts on this.
- I would love to talk to you about how to move _____ forward. I think we may have different ideas about how to _____.
- I wonder if we might reach a better understanding about _____. I really want to hear your feelings about this and share my perspective as well to come up with next steps.

Once the other person has a clear understanding of the issue you want to discuss and what you hope to resolve, lead with open-ended questions to clarify and align around your issue. You can accomplish this by asking and listening to the response to questions like the following:

- What do you see as the main issue?
- Do you see the issue differently?

- From where you sit, do you believe this is a problem?
- Do you think this is an important issue?
- How would you describe the issue in this situation?
- What would you like to resolve in this conversation?

Once you have heard the other's perspective on what the issue is for your HSC, there will be space for sharing how you see the issue if it has not already been addressed. Perhaps, multiple central issues will surface. Hold onto all of them and decide what is the most important to tackle first.

The act of defining the issue not only focuses the parties on what you will solve, but it also establishes your first piece of common ground, even if it is a problem to solve. Peace negotiators working with foreign nations use this technique—to first identify areas of agreement before tackling their differences.

High-Stakes Conversation
Step #2: Explore Perspectives

This is the step where Quality Questions are used the most. Go back and review Chapter 9 if needed to ensure you are comfortable with the key components of Quality Questions.

You have probably heard of the old Indian parable about the blind men and the elephant. This is a story of a group of blind men who touch an elephant to learn what it is like. Each one feels a different but singular part, such as its side, tusk, or tail. They then compare perspectives and learn that they are in complete disagreement with each other's description of the elephant, as is shown in Figure 10.1.

Each man is partly right, as each has touched one major part of the elephant. However, they are all wrong, because in their limited perspectives, they failed to comprehend the creature in its entirety. Their description is missing other important information that can only be gained by effective communication and respect for the other men's perspectives.

A similar dynamic can occur when you're trying to advance your MTM through an HSC. You will need to understand others' perspectives, insights, knowledge, and skills. You do not need to agree with others'

Figure 10.1 The blind men and the elephant

"truths," but awareness of the relevant perspectives enables you to more accurately view the MTM. Best case, you learn a deeper perspective for moving forward. Those who are best at HSCs understand that different experiences, access to information, values, goals, personalities, and perceptions often lead to novel conclusions and insights.

Imagine that you are leading the six men and the elephant, trying to get to the bottom of what those men touched. You would want to dig deeper, asking open-ended questions to gain each man's perspective along with their collective understanding of what they felt when they touched the elephant. Likewise, in your MTM, ask open-ended Quality Questions to increase information and trust.

Following are examples of open-ended Quality Questions for understanding others' perspectives about the issue. HSCs are dynamic, so while preparing questions in advance can be helpful, you will need to stay in the moment, asking Quality Questions and sharing constructively throughout. The Quality Questions listed can serve as a guide.

Sample Quality Questions for Exploring Perspectives

- What is working?
- What is not working?
- What is difficult about this situation from your perspective?
- How do you believe this situation sets you or others up for failure—or success?

- What do you think are the causes?
- What constraints (time, resources, energy, focus, etc.) does this situation present for you?
- How does this situation impact your success?
- Who else is involved in this? What are their expectations?
- How do you feel this issue impacts others?
- What do we know so far or still need to learn about this issue?

High-Stakes Conversation
Step #3: Generate Forward-Focused Solutions

Up to this point, you have clarified the issue to be solved and increased understanding of how others view it. You have demonstrated empathy, generated trust, and discovered perception gaps between you and the other person around the central issue. Now comes a strategic shift within your HSC where the focus moves away from current perspectives about the issue and begins focusing on future possibilities for improvement and growth.

Stay Solution Oriented

If you stay in the issue too long, it is easy to feel disempowered or like all doors are shut.

"We've got an issue...oh no! Not another issue!" You are bound to get weary if you stay stuck. Strategically shifting the focus toward solutions frees your mindset toward what is possible.

Once you better understand the other person's perspective, look for the right opportunity to shift the focus from the problem to the solution. This is where everyone receives the pay-off of investing in understanding each other's perspectives. It is tempting to go straight to problem-solving for future solutions, but without groundwork clarity on the issue and understanding of how each person perceives the issue, problem-solving is bound to fail.

It is important to first find common ground for a desired outcome. You may not be able to find perfect alignment on what success looks like for your issue, but usually, there is some area of overlap about desired outcomes that can be found. Finding this agreement is important because it gives everyone in HSC a common purpose to attain when providing possible solutions. It also puts all parties on the same side of the issue. Following are some examples of Quality Questions to define a shared purpose or goals for your HSC.

- What would success look like for you?
- What would you consider an ideal outcome?
- What do you need to consider this a success?

If their desired goals align with yours, acknowledge the agreement and move forward to finding solutions. This is the "sweet spot" for your HSC. If you can get to this point, you and your conversation partner are working together to find solutions to address your MTM. You are no longer on different sides of the issue but are partnering to define next steps. Continue the momentum by leading with Quality Questions that generate forward-focused solutions. See some following examples:

- How would you suggest we move forward?
- What are your ideas for next steps?
- How can we work together to make progress?
- What would you suggest we do if there were no constraints?
- What do you need from me for us to be successful?
- What challenges might come our way, and how might we meet them?

If there is no obvious overlap for shared solutions, look for opportunities for compromise. You can only compromise once you have asked Quality Questions and listened intently for desired outcomes. What overlapping interests or needs can you focus on moving forward? This will build trust and momentum for small wins together, so you can address more contentious future issues. Following are some statements to offer compromise and move forward:

- Let us agree to include both of our views in a solution…
- The part I agree with is…
- I agree with much of what you are saying and….
- Let us find a compromise here
- I think there may be some common ground between us in this aspect.
- Yes, and…
- How can we create a win–win situation?

What If There Is No Common Ground for Solutions?

Usually, if you commit to engaging others in an HSC, you will find alignment and shared "next steps" to improve the MTM situation. But not always. Unfortunately, there are times when the people involved cannot find enough common ground to create shared solutions or next steps. This inability to align occurs primarily for one of the following two reasons.

1. *The context of the situation does not allow for a win–win.* For one individual or group to win, the other group must lose or take less. One time in Scott's career, a peer in another department "suggested" that Scott transfer several of his employees to the department of this peer. As both departments had different goals and deliverables, had Scott agreed to "donate" his staff, he would have compromised his ability to remain successful in meeting the goals of his department. Needless to say, Scott declined his peer's "generous" offer.

2. *Individuals have incongruent core values.* Think about the hot topics of religion, gun control, abortion, politics, and so on. These topics hit areas where most people are not willing to look for common ground. Have you ever successfully changed someone's mind on any of these topics? A card-carrying member of People for the Ethical Treatment of Animals (PETA) and lifelong vegetarian will never feel comfortable working in a slaughterhouse. One set of values falls in direct conflict with another.

This is a time where you will need to agree to escalate the issue if there is a higher-level authority. If not, you will just need to agree to disagree and walk away with an increased understanding of why this issue exists and additional insights for what that means for you to succeed with your MTM.

Scott: Taking a Stand on Values

While it's not common, you might come across times when you cannot create a win–win or negotiate around incongruous core values.

When Scott worked as a crisis counselor for a private organization delivering counseling services to the state of Michigan, he had many hoops to jump through for compliance relating to timeliness of family visits and paperwork.

Early in his career, Scott faxed his new client paperwork to the main office. For whatever reason, the fax did not get submitted to the state file before an upcoming state audit. Scott's boss, Jade, called him a few days later. During the call, Jade reminded Scott that their contract was very specific about the timeliness requirement and potential consequence of being noncompliant (i.e., loss of the contract). Then, Jade asked Scott to send the documents again, but she asked Scott to back-date and mail them so they would appear to have been delayed by the postal service instead of lost in the office or eaten by the fax machine.

Had Scott complied with Jade's request, he would be falsifying records, something that could lead to his immediate termination. If he didn't comply, he could be found noncompliant and potentially lose the state contract.

Scott didn't have to think about it. He told Jade, "No." He explained that Jade could fire him, but he would not falsify the reports. Scott went on to explain that if he were willing to falsify reports provided to the state, how could Jade ever know that he was not falsifying expense reports or mileage reports that he submitted to Jade?

Jade didn't fire Scott, nor did they lose the contract. Scott took a stand that to him was important enough to risk his job over.

Fortunately, most situations don't ask you to quit or face termination.

Even if you cannot align on the same desired outcome or perception of the issue, the investment in understanding each other's views will help everyone decide on the best way forward. As an added bonus, you also will have increased understanding of how to engage in future interactions with these individuals. This experience will build a foundation for potential partnership. A worst-case scenario is that you have clearly identified a context where you and others have incongruent perspectives and goals, which allows you to proactively define useful mitigation strategies to co-exist or exit this engagement.

High-Stakes Conversation
Step #4: Take Shared Action

You will greatly benefit by understanding perspectives, intentions, and solutions of another person, but that's not enough to get you the full benefit of your MTM. There is nothing more frustrating than going through all that effort only to have nothing happen, nothing change. No action, no improvement, no advancing your MTM.

The end-goal of conducting an HSC is to create actions for solutions. To accomplish that, your conversation must move into an action plan where accountability is clearly defined. Once you agree about at least some of the solutions, it is time to get moving on them—which requires that everyone do their part.

Following are some Quality Questions to help generate shared accountability for action.

- What are we each committing to do moving forward?
- What steps must we take to get there?
- What piece of this will you own? What piece of this do you believe I should own?
- How will we hold ourselves accountable? How can we hold each other accountable?
- How and when will we reconnect to check progress?

If the solution to your issue involves several moving parts, consider documenting your answers and sharing them in a file with due dates and assignments for who owns which parts. Set a date to follow up to check in on progress and reassess what might need to be adjusted. If it's a simple set of actions, you may be able to rely on verbal agreements only. You be the judge. From our experience, it does not hurt to document, especially when developing new habits or ways forward.

Positive change and advancement of your MTM might not happen in one conversation, as most complex situations usually aren't solved in one conversation. And, most require some compromise to meet in the middle (see sidebar). Be patient and focus on the progress and evolution of your and the other's thinking, not just the immediate short-term outcome. (Remember: apply long-term goals aligned with immediate intentions.)

Willingness to Compromise

Progress toward your MTM often requires compromise between people with conflicting or differing intentions or goals.

Carlos and Ingrid have been married for six years, and they've had the same arguments over those six years. Their biggest disagreement is about how to spend their vacation time.

Ingrid likes vacations that create lasting memories; Carlos prefers a "staycation" where they stay at home, order in, and watch TV. Every year, Carlos and Ingrid ask for 10 days off work from early to mid-July. Ingrid researches places she would like to go and shares them with Carlos starting in April. Carlos finds an excuse for every possible vacation idea (Puerto Rico? *No, they have the Zika Virus!* Dominican Republic? *No, too many tourist deaths and sicknesses!* Hawaii? *The flight is too long!* Florida? *Too crowded!* Chicago? *Gang violence!*). After a short conversation, Carlos asks, "Can't you just be happy with what we have here at home? You're the one that's always complaining about spending too much money!" And the sparks fly.

This ongoing argument is actually an MTM begging for an HSC using Quality Questions. What makes this couple view this situation as a fight is that each of them has predictable triggers, repeats the same mistakes, and accomplishes the same outcomes.

Remember, your MTM is an opportunity to Get It Right, even if you have historically gotten it wrong.

If you are honest with yourself, you don't want to be triggered, trigger your spouse, or go to bed mad. You want to feel heard, respected, and validated. And, the best outcome would be a compromise that both of you can live with. Neither of those goals can be accomplished by doing what you have always done.

Were Carlos and Ingrid to engage in Quality Questions and the four steps of an HSC, in which they listened to one another's perspectives and came up with shared solutions and an action plan, they could likely find success and avoid their repetitive fights on the topic of money. But up to this point, the only question Carlos or Ingrid asks is to themselves: *Why did I marry this person?*

So let us add some Quality Questions. Since reading a book, *Getting It Right When It Matters Most,* Ingrid tries a different approach.

When Carlos comes home from work, Ingrid is already in the kitchen cooking.

"Hey, babe," she says. "What do you think about going for a walk together after dinner? (Okay, it is not exactly an open-ended question, but this Yes/No question allows her to evaluate the timing of her planned HSC.)"

"Sure," Carlos answers. "Nothing good on TV."

As they begin their walk after dinner, Ingrid asks, "Have you already put in your request to take time off in July?" (Again, it is a Yes/No question, but it is a way to open the conversation.)

"I sure have," Carlos answers. "How about you?"

"I have, too," Ingrid says. "And I'm really looking forward to getting away for a while."

Carlos says nothing, so Ingrid continues.

"Carlos, if you were to look at a map of the world, where would you most like to visit?" Ingrid asks him.

"I know where you're going with this," he answers suspiciously. "My favorite place is home."

"Have you ever thought about going somewhere you have read about but never seen?" she asks. "Like Spain to visit the town where your grandparents came from? Or maybe go see the Roman Forum in real life instead of on TV?"

"Yeah, it'd be nice, but you know I don't like to travel. It costs too much, takes too long to get there, we speak only English, and we don't have passports," he told her as if he had done his "excuse homework."

"How about in this country? Remember that show we watched about the Grand Canyon? And that other one about Yosemite National Park? Wouldn't you love to see something like that?" she responded, taking to heart some of his objections.

"Ingrid," he said patiently, "I just like to stay home, eat, watch TV. You know, keep things simple and relaxing."

"I know, Carlos," Ingrid said as she breathed. "But I'd like to suggest a compromise. For the last six years, we've taken our vacations at home. I would like to stay at home one year, and then go away the next. That way we could save up, plan something fun and special, and have a chance to experience something together that neither of us has seen before."

"That's why we have cable," Carlos answered dismissively.

"Let me back up for a minute," Ingrid said as she thought through her best intention. "Carlos, my desire to go away and take a vacation somewhere with you is to get closer to you. When we watch TV, which is fine, we aren't talking. We're listening to someone else talk. Our honeymoon was wonderful, because it was just the two of us, disconnected for a while, doing things together. I want to get closer to you, Carlos. Does that make sense?"

"So," Carlos answered, "Let me see if I got this straight. You want to get closer to me in a way that we can't do when we stay home, eating, and watching TV together?"

Ingrid smiled. "That's exactly what I want. And I'll tell you what: you can pick the place. I'll do all the planning. We can make decisions together if you like. And then next year, we can plan a staycation and rotate."

Maybe this sounds unrealistic, but it is very similar to a conversation that one of the authors had with his spouse. No one wants to be seen as selfish. When someone cares enough to listen to your objections, consider them, and try to address them, reasonable people will listen.

And, by the way, one of the authors who is the inspiration for Carlos in this story is going to Wales with his spouse next year. It works!

Practice Makes Progress

If the HSC calls for it, you could ask a friend to help you conduct an extended role play to practice what you are going to say and engage in active listening, handling resistance, and keeping the conversation neutral, solution-focused, and positive. That process could take a few minutes or several hours, which is worth it to create a successful outcome. You can right size these concepts to best fit your needs.

You have now spent time learning about the most essential aspects of Self, Outlook, and Action. Using the skills we have shared up to this point, you are equipped to engage in your HSCs. But remember that SOAR is a dynamic cycle, and you may revisit chapters to refresh yourself on how to use specific skills as you need them. In fact, during your HSC, you may need to practice your pause and breathe techniques frequently.

CHAPTER 11

Managing Negative Reactions in Your High-Stakes Conversations

If "ifs" and "ands" were pots and pans There would be no need for tinker's hands!

—Scottish nursery rhyme

Going Down the Rabbit Hole

After Scott's daughter, Alana, watched *Star Wars* for the first time, he found her with her hand outstretched toward a coffee table.

"What are you doing?" Scott asked.

"I'm trying to make my book come to me," she answered honestly.

"You're trying to see…?" he started to ask.

"If I'm a Jedi!" she finished his question without embarrassment.

Alas, we are not Jedis. Well, maybe you are, but the authors admit readily that they do not have the power to bend the laws of physics or control minds. And, unless you have those supernatural powers, you will need to apply some of the tips we have already covered when your well-intended High-Stakes Conversation (HSC) goes down the rabbit hole into a place you hoped to avoid.

Outlook and Your High-Stakes Conversation Partners

Your Outlook comes with you wherever you go. In the Outlook phase of the SOAR self-leadership cycle, we explored the cognitive biases that join your MTMs and can distort perceptions of the situation, yourself, and others in your HSCs. We spent so much time on how to stretch your Outlook and perceptions, so they do not become static.

Just like you have an Outlook about other people, other people have an Outlook about you! Each HSC involves multiple Outlooks. When you add important, complex, and relational situations, you add threats, fears of potential loss, and heightened emotions.

While your Outlook should stretch and be portable, you may find yourself in MTMs with the following categories of people.

1. *Those you have known for a long time.* The more time you spend with another person, the greater the likelihood your relationship has experienced a time of mistrust, negative judgments, disappointments, or betrayal. This does not mean anyone is bad or has ill intent; it just means that you have experienced the ups and downs of any human relationship.

2. *Someone with whom you would not normally engage.* When you share an interest, you may need to engage in an HSC to achieve your desired goal. Sometimes, this is with someone you would not otherwise communicate with. For example, some divorced couples need HSCs around child visitation or childcare issues. While neither party may wish to engage, an HSC is often the only way to ensure the best interest of their children are served.

3. *A relative stranger.* If your child's principal or someone from HR were to call you for a meeting, you most likely just got served an MTM with someone you don't know well. You didn't go looking for it, but it found you.

While you can choose your own Outlook, you cannot always choose your HSC partners—or their Outlook or baggage. Those factors can make conversations messy and challenging—quickly deteriorating into interactions that derail progress in your MTM.

Managing Negative Reactions

If the person in your HSC reacts negatively, it's likely that the situation or your conversation has triggered their threat response. Something about the HSC or MTM situation has made them feel psychologically unsafe.

Remember the ARC (Autonomy, Relationships, Competence) model for motivation and threat in Chapter 5? People react, often with

Table 11.1 Fight-or-flight responses

FLIGHT RESPONSE	FIGHT RESPONSE
Accommodating	Controlling
Silence/Avoiding	Attacking
Ignoring	Fighting
Shutting Down	Debating

defensiveness, when they perceive a threat to their ARC needs. Considering the flight or fight mode, these behaviors inhibit problem-solving, creativity, and collaboration (see Table 11.1).

Most of our focus has been on preparing your Self and Outlook to engage in the Action of HSCs. We have deliberately focused on what you can control, because doing so empowers you in your MTMs.

What you cannot control is *other people's reactions*. The remainder of this chapter will focus on what you *can* control when other people react, especially with defensiveness, so your HSC does not get derailed. These strategies will help you diffuse pressure and re-align on what matters.

Forms of Defensiveness: A Case Study

Imagine that while you work from home during the COVID-19 outbreak, a senior leader charges you and a colleague, Jill, to update your business continuity plan so your organization is better prepared for subsequent crises. The senior leader makes it clear that "this is your top and only priority," and you are given two weeks to turn in your first draft for review.

You and Jill divide up sections and tasks for completing a review of the current continuity plan. You offered to write up the new table of contents, create a short summary, and highlight all recommended changes. The two of you agreed to share documents online so you can complete your parts of the work simultaneously.

But Jill has not shared any documents for three days. You have emailed and called her several times, and her response is always the same: "I'm uploading the new documents now." And still, you have not seen anything. You become very concerned that the report is due on Monday. Today is Thursday. Even if you got all the documents you needed within the hour, you will have to work all weekend long to make the final version ready.

After lunch on Thursday, Jill emails you to say that she is running behind, but hopes to have something to you by the end of business Friday.

Now you find yourself in the middle of an MTM, so you take it as an opportunity to have an HSC.

You call Jill, saying something like this, "Jill, I'm concerned about being able to get things done on my side even if I had all of your updates today. Can we talk about how we can work together to deliver this report on time?" Table 11.2 shows her possible defensive responses.

You know that your statement and question is fine. You thought through it before you spoke. And you are pretty sure that you kept out any negative voice tone, even though you feel threatened by the approaching deadline. But you are also frustrated because you finished your half of the work with no problem. As you offered to do the tasks that would come at the very end of the work, you are feeling screwed over.

None of that matters at this point, because how Jill responds now is up to her.

Have you ever seen any of these reactions? We know you have. Now to add to your own self-awareness, which response do you have when

Table 11.2 *Defensive reactions*

Anger	"I didn't ask to be on this project. Since you're the senior person, I assumed that you'd be doing much more of the work than me."
Excuses	"It's a madhouse over here. I'm home schooling three boys...." "No one told my other clients that I'm on a special project, so I've had to help them. I don't have time to do both." "I never thought that two weeks was enough time to get all of this done...."
Denial	"All you have to do is cut and paste once I send it to you. It's not going to be a big deal. A couple of hours, and you're done."
Deflecting humor	"Do you think the boss would believe my dog ate my laptop?"
Blaming	"I've never liked this document sharing platform. Thanks to IT, I've spent more time trying to figure out how to use this software than actually working on the report...." "You gave me the longest sections of the report, so of course it's going to take me longer to get this done!"
Passive aggression	"We can talk about it if you want, but it's just going to take me longer to get you my material if we waste time talking about it."
Sarcasm	"If you've found a way to slow down time, I'm all ears!"

triggered or defensive? Each of us has a natural reaction. Knowing your tendency equips you to manage the reactions of yourself and others.

Which leads to the next point: What are the best strategies for managing defensive reactions?

The Five A's for Managing Defensive Reactions

Have you ever said something that you believed to be innocently worded and in a neutral voice, only to have the other person react like a tiger about to pounce? It happens all the time with our spouses, children, coworkers, and bosses. At times, the other person detected something you said or the way you said it and felt triggered (Table 11.3).

Were you a gifted Jedi, you could read minds, plant thoughts, and change others' reactions. Instead of using those superpowers, you must rely on what you see through observation and hear through words and tone.

The very nature of some HSCs can make others feel threatened. One thing is clear: you won't have ongoing success with your HSCs unless you can understand what is threatening others and create a safe space for a productive dialogue. Following are the five A's for addressing defensive reactions so you can get back on track with having a quality HSC.

Address Your Negative Emotions

What happens when you give constructive criticism or feedback to a person whose natural response is blaming, minimizing, shifting focus, or

Table 11.3 Defensive interpretations

What you said...	What the other person may hear...
Did you get my email?	You think I never read my email.
When should I expect that report?	You think I am slacking on the report.
Is everything okay?	You think I look pissed off.
Did you get a haircut?	You hate my haircut.
How should we move forward?	You want me to change to accommodate you.
I think we both agree that...	You have decided for both of us...
Can we talk about this situation?	You are upset with me around this situation.
I am excited to work with you again!	You will take credit for my work again!

shutting down? If your reaction is *flight*, you may stop giving that person feedback. You may even avoid that person altogether. But if your response is *fight*, it's likely that you will react with your own defensiveness, which only escalates negative feelings and conflict.

We have all experienced the negative impact of reacting out of fear or anger. Later we often regret that we were not more in control of our emotions, words, and actions.

In Chapter 6, we shared "Three Mindfulness Strategies to Regulate Emotions." It may have seemed theoretical, as it was far removed from any confrontation. But, as you enter an HSC with the very real possibility of a negative reaction, it bears repeating.

While you are not always afforded the luxury of scheduling impromptu HSCs, you learned how your body reacts when negative emotions are triggered (e.g., clenched jaw, shallow increased breathing, a sinking feeling in your stomach, and maybe starting to feel hot or sweat). Then recall the Three Mindfulness Strategies to Regulate Emotions that we covered in Chapter 6.

Pause

Speaking when you are angry is a great way to make the best speech you will forever regret. How do you stifle the urge to react defensively instead of respond thoughtfully? Pause.

Before entering your HSC, set your intention *not* to react to others' defensiveness. Think through worst-case responses by the other person. Practice pausing after hearing those things. Then pause when or if they actually happen. If you discipline yourself to create space between your negative emotions and action, you have already won.

Breathe

After you Pause, regain emotional equilibrium through your breath. If you feel your HSC partner's reaction triggering negative emotions, and you feel anger or fear, breathe to regain control. You now know that your emotions mimic your breathing, so calm your emotions by taking slow, deep breaths. Remember that a 4:6 inhale to exhale ratio is recommended. Using this breathing technique, even for one or two cycles when you sense negative emotions building, helps calm you to choose your response. As your brain settles down, choose to be curious about why the person reacted to you so aggressively.

Label Your Feelings

Identify how you are feeling and put those feelings into words. Labeling your emotions immediately diminishes the power of negative feelings. Research shows this practice greatly improves well-being and enhancing decision making. As neuroscientist say, "name it to tame it". Labeling an emotion diffuses its power.

After you have paused, breathed, and labeled your feelings, ask yourself: *What is my best intention in this HSC?* When calm and composed, you won't think about scoring a point, being right, or putting down the other person. Instead, you remind yourself to be level-headed. When Your Best Self shows up, you want to help the other person join you in a place of calm. Your best intention is to find common ground and come to a resolution that works for both parties.

Acknowledge and Validate the Other's Negative Emotions

Every party brings emotions to the interaction. While positive emotions unleash creativity, negative emotions inhibit listening, processing of information, and problem-solving. So, just as you regained control over your own negative emotions, you need to acknowledge that the other person has emotions too. Unless you manage the emotional part of the conversation, you will not get back on track.

If you've ever tried to minimize or dismiss the negative emotions of another person, you've likely learned that it actually amplifies them! Has saying to your spouse or significant other something like, "Calm down," "Don't cry," or "Stop that," when he or she is triggered ever worked? Never in the history of a heated discussion have similar phrases done anything except add fuel to already hot emotions. Those phrases can be interpreted as code for, "I don't understand or care about or your feelings, and I refuse to validate what you're expressing." Not the basis for a successful HSC, right?

Also, we don't always interpret others' emotions accurately. It's important not to assume we know what the other person feels—or to label them—but instead to ask for clarity or validation of your observations.

Try a couple of the following statements to demonstrate that you heard or saw (in their body language) that the other person is angry, hurt, upset, or frustrated:

- It sounds like you're feeling (frustrated, upset, surprised, etc.).
  Is that correct?
- Tell me if I've got this straight. You feel _____ because...
- Thank you for being open and sharing your feelings with me.
  I really appreciate it and now have a better understanding
  of...
- I'm sorry that I didn't fully understand how you were feeling
  about _____ until now, and I'm grateful that you've shared
  this with me.
- I can see why you would think that...
- That isn't what I meant, but I can see how you could take it
  that way...

Start from a position that accepts what the other person perceives, feels, and says is *valid for them, is about them, and comes from their own reality*. At times, the person may be projecting negative emotions based on how someone made them feel in the past. Even if that is true, understand that the quickest way to diffuse and diminish emotional intensity is to let the other person express those feelings. Remember what Google research found? Teams that create psychological safety outperform other teams. The same is true of you. When you create a safe space to express negative emotions, you set the stage for a meaningful conversation.

Note that this works only when you are interacting with someone who is not abusive to you. In a chronically abusive relationship wherein someone is only trying to win or put you down, these tactics will not work. You will know a relationship is abusive if you are called names, belittled, railroaded, dismissed, and gaslighted—without progress ever made or compromise occurring. We recommend putting yourself in a place of safety and finding a therapist to work on next steps if this is the case. Depending on the relationship, it may be time to walk away—or set strong boundaries if you need to continue interacting.

Ask Follow-Up Questions about the Other's Negative Emotions

Once you have acknowledged and validated the other person's feelings, ask follow-up questions to dig deeper. Following is a short list of examples to give you more insight:

- I am listening. Can you tell me more about that?
- What makes you say that?
- Can you share more about that?
- Do you have an example that might help me better understand?

Get comfortable with asking follow-up questions, then being patient with silence so that you can listen to a response.

What If They Are Defensive Because of Something You Said?

If the person reacts defensively to something you said, ask follow-up questions to understand why they interpreted your words as a threat, criticism, or judgment. Try to understand how it could have been taken the wrong way and acknowledge that. Then explain what you really meant.

If the other person misunderstood your intent, clarify by saying: "I did mean to say this _____, but I didn't mean to say this _____."

If you misspoke, admit that you did not express your perspective as clearly as you would have liked. Apologize for creating confusion.

Power of Apologies

Business coach and best-selling author of more than 35 books, Marshall Goldsmith says this about the power of the apology:

"I regard apologizing as the most magical, healing, restorative gesture human beings can make. It is the centerpiece of my work with executives who want to get better," says Marshall Goldsmith in *What Got You Here Won't Get You There*. The centerpiece of his coaching with executives is not on how to be right, how to show others how smart you are, or how to get your way. He teaches leaders how to apologize and own up to their mistakes.

If you have offended someone with something you have said or done, apologize sincerely. Period. That short phrase, "I'm sorry" is one of the most challenging yet beneficial statements a leader will ever make.

Nowhere in your best intention should there be a desire to Be Right at all costs or make someone feel bad. For success in your HSCs, you need the other person to work with you. This can happen when you hear, address, and remove any unintended confusion as soon as you recognize it.

Agree on How to Move Forward in the High-Stakes Conversation

You might need a time-out to regain emotional balance. Once both parties are ready to move forward, it is time to find common ground for continuing your HSC.

One way to get back on track after a defensive reaction is to ask what the other needs from you and share your needs to move forward in the HSC. Finding common ground and making agreements is a great first step to regaining trust and momentum.

The following statements can help you forge an agreement with your HSC partner:

- Yes, I agree. And _____.
- Let's find a compromise here by _____.

- I agree with part of what you are saying, and

  _____.

- I think there may be some common ground between us in this aspect.
- Let's agree to include both of our views in a solution.

Align Around Common Ground and Shared Goals

In Chapter 7, we shared the importance of aligning your long-term goals and in-the-moment intentions. This same principle applies when your HSC goes sideways. When others are defensive without an apparent reason to be triggered, stop talking about the issue and revisit your shared goals. See if the HSC is still focused on addressing the agreements you made in Step 1 of your HSC: Align on the issue(s) and outcome. If not, why? Has the conversation gone off on a tangent? Do you need to revisit your agreements about the issue or reevaluate the outcome, because it is no longer applicable?

If alignment no longer exists, agree on an updated core issue and outcome of your HSC. Alignment on the issue and outcome should extend across the entirety of your HSC. Where there is mutual understanding—and outcomes are known, aligned, and shared—there is mutual buy-in for success.

In short... When you have an HSC with someone who is reactive, practice the five A's:

- *A*djust your own negative feelings
- *A*cknowledge and validate the other's feelings
- *A*sk follow-up questions about those emotions
- *A*gree on how to move forward in the HSC
- *A*lign around common ground and shared goals

Practicing these five A's keeps your HSCs moving forward even if they run into resistance early on.

Let's Sit on It

Sometimes, walking away from a situation for a while is a useful way to solve it later.

Lynn's husband, David, does not need a lot of social time. He is an introvert who is happiest when reading a book or listening to music. Lynn is the opposite. She recharges her battery while with others: family, friends, neighbors, and even strangers. So, Lynn has learned David has a quick, automatic answer ready to any suggested social visit: "No."

Fortunately for their relationship, Lynn understands that David's "No" right now usually becomes "We'll see" in a couple days, "I guess" in a week, and "Okay" by the time the social gathering begins. What does Lynn have to do to change David's mind? Nothing. David's automatic reaction to the thought of putting on shoes, leaving the house, and making small talk with strangers is his nature. Because David knows that spending time with friends is important to Lynn, he usually complies without extra fuss—and ironically seems to enjoy it!

The point is, not every negative reaction needs to be solved or addressed in real time. In fact, forcing the issue or pushing for closure can actually backfire. If Lynn begged David each day to reconsider, her action could look to David like *nagging*. Nagging works really well—to create resentment!

If your HSC is met with pushback, sometimes your best response is to take a time-out to pause, breathe, and recall your best intention before re-engaging. And, in some situations, a longer pause can provide new perspectives and solutions.

Depending on the MTM, you may work toward a solution once you work through these reactions. Or you may need to walk away until emotions settle and each person can re-face the situation with a fresh perspective.

As mentioned earlier, some people are abusive by nature. These people will not seek a peaceful, joint resolution to any particular problem. Rather, they solicit a verbal sparring partner to bait into an argument. Your MTM or HSC will fail with these individuals. You will need to find another approach for success.

Action: Self-Assessment and Review

Now that you have finished reading the *Action phase*, read the following statements (Table 11.4) and assess your current proficiency using the following scale:

Table 11.4 *Action: Self-assessment and review*

5—Strongly agree

4—Agree

3—Neither agree nor disagree

2—Disagree

1—Strongly agree

1.	When entering an HSC, I am always clear about my best intentions (Results and Relationships) for the conversation.	5	4	3	2	1
2.	I always try to create clarity and alignment on the core issue in my HSCs.	5	4	3	2	1
3.	I lead with open-ended questions in my HSCs to understand others' perspectives.	5	4	3	2	1
4.	I take time to ask follow-up questions in my HSCs to increase my understanding.	5	4	3	2	1
5.	I am comfortable allowing space and silence after asking a question in my HSCs.	5	4	3	2	1
6.	I always come prepared to share my perspectives on the issue in my HSCs.	5	4	3	2	1
7.	I create space for listening and sharing my perspectives during my HSCs.	5	4	3	2	1
8.	I know how to ask questions that generate forward-focused solutions in my HSCs.	5	4	3	2	1
9.	I always make time to develop clear agreements for shared action before leaving an HSC.	5	4	3	2	1
10.	I am comfortable with handling defensiveness of others during HSCs.	5	4	3	2	1
11.	I know how to manage my defensive feelings during HSCs.	5	4	3	2	1

Before moving on to the *Reflection phase*, consider making an action plan for any scores that fall lower than a 4 on these statements. Scores of 3 or below represent where you are most vulnerable to *getting it wrong* in your MTMs.

PART IV

Reflection

The SOAR model—Reflection

CHAPTER 12

Practice Reflection

Follow effective action with quiet reflection. From the quiet reflection will come even more effective action.

—Peter Drucker

While we have covered a lot of ground, we are not done yet. Yes, you have the skills. But how do you apply what you have learned to accelerate your fluency? The way you do it is to practice Reflection. Read on to learn more…

Imagine what it would be like if you couldn't learn from the experiences you encountered? Fortunately, you *can*. By actively practicing Reflection after you act, you perpetually create "lessons learned" for the actions you should repeat—and the ones to change.

We will now shift focus to the phase of the SOAR cycle that accelerates your capacity to continually adapt, learn, and grow: Reflection.

Practicing Reflection for the Next Journey

The sailing crew experienced more important moments throughout their trip, enhancing their learning. Their ongoing learning would be critical, because they still had to sail from the Bahamas back to Florida—a new goal! Before heading back to the United States, they practiced Reflection. They shared feedback and asked questions to grow and learn for future Action, such as:

- What do we need to repeat on the way home?
- How can we work together more effectively?
- What contingencies should we make before leaving?
- What mistakes can we avoid on our way back?

With all these components in place, the crew did SOAR back to Florida, with their sails flying high. They completed their journey—safely and effectively—and began planning their next trip.

Reflection—or the process of critically evaluating how behaviors served you in accomplishing a goal—has been identified by numerous researchers as crucial to any learning process. When reflecting, one considers an experience and tries to understand it, which often leads to insight and deep learning—or ideas to test on new experiences.

Reflection can lead to course correction, which can drive meaningful change. "Understanding how to implement the process of course correction increases a leader's influence, which enables the organization to do more good in the world," states Marlene Chism in *No Drama Leadership*. "Eventually the leader's influence has the capacity to transform not only the workplace but the community, the country, and the world at large" (Chism 2016).

You do not have the time or energy to Reflect about every interaction. If you did this, you would never get anything done! But it is critical to "think about your thinking" after your most important, complex, and relational situations so that you can adjust. Your MTM situations are leverage points to grow from your experiences. Reflection is most necessary when you are struggling, confused, experiencing emotional pain, or run into roadblocks. These are all common feelings after encountering your MTMs. These are the situations when Reflection is most necessary to succeed in your current and future MTMs.

Scott: Team Debrief

For years, Scott led a team responsible for, among other things, coordinating large, nationwide leadership conferences within his organization. At the end of each conference, Scott would call his team together to conduct what he called "postmortems" to debrief the events. Eventually, Scott realized that the name *postmortem* implied that "the meeting died, and I want to know who killed it!" He soon changed the name to "lessons learned," stressing that every situation is a learning opportunity to share both things that went well and those that can go better next time.

Scott attributes the success of his team in assuming larger, more complicated events to the use of team Reflection.

Experience Is the Best Teacher

Experience is the hardest kind of teacher. It gives you the test first and the lesson afterward.

—Anonymous

By age three, Scott's son Jack understood the meaning of almost everything his parents said. But Jack often seemed to crave more than information; he wanted *proof*. So, after hearing his mother say, "No, don't touch the burner. It's very hot," he complied—until his mom turned her back. Then he reached his hand to the burner and touched it with his fingertips.

Jack learned a valuable lesson that day, and fortunately one that did not scar him for life. Rather, his experience rather boldly underscored the fact that his parents spoke the truth—and the stove, indeed, was very hot!

When Austin, the senior vice president of operations for a multi-billion-dollar company promoted Amy to senior director, he invited her to attend his weekly staff meetings each Monday at 8:30 a.m.

As Amy worked on a different floor, she underestimated the ease of catching an elevator to take her down during the morning rush when every employee seemed to be heading up. As a result, she slipped into Austin's office a few minutes late and found that the meeting had started without her.

When she opened the door, Austin stopped talking and looked at Amy while she found a seat. Then, he offered these stinging words: "If I wanted the meeting to start at 8:35, I would have scheduled it for 8:35."

Guess who never arrived late to another meeting with Austin after that day?

Too often, we assume that learning involves reading books, attending courses, or getting a degree. This perspective dismisses our primary avenue for learning, which is learning through experience. Think back to a time when you learned a lesson that positively impacted you. Now take a couple of seconds to consider where and how you learned.

We have asked thousands of people to consider this same scenario and followed it up with this request: *Raise your hand if you learned your important lesson in a classroom or structured learning situation.* In our experience, it is rare that someone raises a hand to indicate that the important lesson occurred in a formal classroom. This exercise confirms what you already know, which is that your most important lessons as an adult usually come through experience.

Experience Is Part of Learning

John Dewey is attributed as teaching that we learn from reflecting on experience. By focusing on perspectives, habits, assumptions, and communication, we gather insights to adapt to future challenges. Research shows a regular habit of Reflection provides the following benefits:

- Increased self-awareness, emotional intelligence, and capacity for emotional regulation—and as a consequence, the ability to inspire and influence others
- Enhanced ability to make decisions that show good judgment
- Growth in the capacity to innovate through asking Quality Questions and attending to the answers with an open mind
- Heightened compassion for self and others
- Improved capacity to inspire trust through demonstrating trustworthiness

> *Failure is instructive. The person who really thinks learns quite as much from his failures as from his successes.*
>
> —John Dewey

Scott: Reflection Allows for Auto-Correct When We Get It Wrong

As a young social worker, Scott got invited to work with a Native American client with some financial issues. The client's former boyfriend had racked up a 700 U.S. dollars phone bill, and she was unable to get needed phone service to stay in touch with her son who was in a group home 30 miles away. As the client and her son were both under the leadership of the Ojibwe Nation, Scott sat with the chief and other tribal leaders to brainstorm ideas to keep mother and son in contact. Scott had never met with the tribal leaders before, and he was relieved to find that the chief had a wonderful sense of humor.

The brainstorming stalled after a few minutes. Trying to get ideas flowing again, Scott asked, "Do they both know smoke signals?"

Thirty years later, Scott is still mortified that he said that. "You could have heard a pin drop. Here I was an invited guest into this meeting, and I had just made a comment that was in poor taste as well as insensitive. I prayed for a hole to open underneath me and swallow me. Fortunately, after a few moments of silence, the chief laughed and said, "No good. Mom lives in a valley."

What did he learn upon Reflection?

"I often use humor when a conversation gets stuck or I feel uncomfortable. But humor should never cause discomfort. Know your audience. Examine your best intention, and be very sensitive about how your best intentions—actions and words—might be perceived by others. When you're a guest, let others speak first. And if you speak, do so only if you have something positive to contribute," Scott related.

Since that time, Scott has worked with a wide variety of executive corporate leaders, politicians, celebrities, and business owners. In preparation for working with any group, he more often reflects on the painful lessons he has learned along the way than any of his successes.

He summed it up by sharing this: "When we take the time to reflect on our errors, we save ourselves from making the same mistake twice."

The famous Swiss psychiatrist and author Carl Jung said, "Until you make the unconscious conscious, it will direct your life and you will call it fate." It is hard to disagree with this statement.

The Neuroscience Behind Reflective Practice

We know from neuroscience that a structure in the brain called the *corpus callosum* affects our performance. The corpus callosum is a thick band of nerve fibers connecting the left and right sides of the brain, transferring information between the hemispheres. The two hemispheres excel in different functions. The left side controls most analytical thinking, language processing, and drawing on existing knowledge to solve problems. The right side controls intuition, creativity, and understanding through metaphor and visualization. Reflective practice helps us revisit and strengthen the neuronal connections we need to develop new habits or skills or mindsets within and between the two hemispheres. In simple terms, Reflection helps both sides of the brain work together to accelerate future learning. (Produced in collaboration with Grace Owen and Alison Fletcher, *What Is the Difference Between Reflection and Reflective Practice?* https://cipd.co.uk/Images/reflective-practice-guide_tcm18-12524.pdf)

Your ability to be mindful and build your emotional and social skills is dependent upon your practice of Reflection. Bringing Your Best Self to your MTM when the stakes are high, people's behaviors are unpredictable, and there are no clear "right" answers is a difficult task. Fortunately, through a practice of Reflection on your experiences, you can accelerate development in these areas and eventually master critical behaviors for success.

Three Strategies for a Successful Reflection Practice

Developing a deliberate practice of Reflection is essential to personal growth. Everyone will have blind spots, make mistakes, develop bad habits, and need to learn new approaches. Reflection is the tool that accelerates your learning and creates new behaviors for positive change. Following are three strategies for implementing Reflection.

Reflection Strategy #1: Ask for Feedback

Due to the complexity and relational aspects of your MTMs, you will often be the last to know when your well-intended behaviors and actions are causing unintended issues that negatively impact your ability to meet desired goals. How do we prevent this from happening? Ask for feedback.

Few things accelerate your learning as much as actively seeking honest, constructive feedback about your behaviors, actions, and effectiveness (Anseel et al. 2009). This behavior demonstrates your authenticity by showing that you understand you don't have all the answers and are open to adjusting. Really listening and caring about others' feedback builds trust. Feedback also helps you fill in blind spots (as you may recall from the Johari Window) to effectiveness in your actions moving forward.

Spotlight Weakness

"Show your humanity by revealing your mistakes and weaknesses," states Anne Bruce, speaker, coach, and bestselling author of 22 leadership books, including *Leaders—Start to Finish.* "Teach your leaders that knowing and appreciating their own limitations as well as their glories will better equip them to build strong human relationships."

She adds that being vulnerable enough to admit to one's own mistakes and model vulnerability sets the stage for healthy relationships and engagement. Asking others for feedback diminishes threats and sets the stage for others to do the same, as you are "walking the walk." As Anne suggests, you should "never ask others to do anything you wouldn't do" (Bruce 2001).

Research suggests that feedback conversations must begin with the goal of minimizing the threat response. We all know that receiving constructive feedback is hard. Going back to the ARC model, receiving negative feedback will almost immediately trigger a threat to Autonomy, Relationships, or Competence. Left unchecked, this situation can trigger a fight, flight, or freeze response that can damage relationships.

We have all felt the negative feelings from receiving unwanted or negative feedback. But have you ever considered how difficult it is for those who truly want to provide feedback to help others?

Following is research that highlights why feedback is important in the workplace despite it being difficult for both providers and receivers (State of Employee Engagement 2020).

- 62 percent of employees wish they received more feedback from their colleagues.
- 83 percent of employees really appreciate receiving feedback, regardless of if it is positive or negative.

- 96 percent of employees said that receiving feedback regularly is a good thing.
- Four out of 10 workers are actively disengaged when they get little or no feedback.

Feedback is critical to learning, adapting, and being more effective. This need for feedback is heightened in your MTMs, where an effective response is magnified. Part of the MTM definition is that they are complex, meaning there are no clear and easy answers. Sometimes learning is most necessary, not just for succeeding in the moment but also for equipping yourself to navigate the ongoing MTMs throughout your journey. How can you ensure you are receiving the necessary feedback for your success? The answer is to ask for—and receive—feedback!

Given all the built-in constraints of receiving honest regular feedback, actively give permission and express an openness to receive feedback about your behaviors and their impact. This permission is critically important for putting yourself and others in a psychological state where they feel safe to help.

Scott: The Evolving Leader

When I earned a promotion to executive chief-of-staff of operations for a multi-billion-dollar company, I had less face time with my employees, except my direct reports. Realizing that their responsibilities grew concurrent with my own, I knew I needed to be more strategic.

I decided to meet with each of my direct reports one-on-one. In the invitation I sent each of my leaders, I asked to meet with them "to help me become a better leader." My transparency up front made it so no one came into my office afraid or confused about my "real" agenda. Once each leader arrived, I explained my new role and challenges.

To get honest feedback, I transitioned by saying something like this: "As I get pulled into many different things, I can't keep leading the way I have been. I won't have time, especially with everything I must learn. So I'd like your help with telling me *what I can do better to support you.*

Specifically, as I get caught up in other activities, what do you need from me to feel supported and valued?"

Up until that point, I had only guessed what my direct reports would say. Once I asked, I not only found a few overarching themes, but I also built better relationships as I learned how to support them as individuals in meeting their goals.

Asking for feedback is a skill, much like asking Quality Questions. The good news is that in both cases, these skills can be learned.

Be Specific with Feedback Request

Begin your request for feedback with a statement that you value others' perspectives and want to make sure you are doing what is necessary to move this MTM in a positive direction. Following are some examples of how to ask for specific feedback:

- During our last conversation, did you feel like you were heard?
- What do you perceive I am doing that is not helpful in this situation?
- From your perspective, how effective have I been at following through on the agreements we made during our last conversation?
- What else can I do or stop doing to improve this situation?

Ask for Feedback Often

Most MTM situations have many interactions including High-Stakes Conversations (HSCs) with follow-through agreements. Ask others for feedback about how they perceive you being a partner in improving the MTM situation. As this becomes part of your regular routine, others will feel safe with offering you feedback. If they believe they were heard the last time they shared feedback, they will develop confidence that you are using the feedback for continuous improvement during your MTMs.

Avoid Defensiveness

Defensiveness about your MTMs comes easily, because they are important and complex, creating an environment where if you feel things are not going well, you can easily be triggered into emotional reaction. The quickest way to ensure you will never hear the truth is to act defensively when you get it. If you are perceived as defensive or denying the other person's perspective, you make a statement that others' feedback is not wanted or valued. Even if you disagree or feel the feedback is unfair, you should ask questions to clarify and thank the person for the candor and willingness to share. Reacting will not make things better for you or others.

Reflection Strategy #2: Answer "What? So What? Now What?"

Gary Rolfe's reflective model is one of the simplest approaches to Reflection, because it centers around asking three simple questions: "What? So what? Now what?" This practical framework guides you to assess past experience, make meaning of it, and assign meaning for future Action (Rolfe et al. 2001).

The "What? So What? Now What?" Reflection model also steers you away from asking *why* questions and focusing on the more useful *what* questions.

- *Why* questions draw focus to your limitations; *what* questions help you see your potential.
- *Why* questions stir up negative emotions; *what* questions keep you curious.
- *Why* questions trap you in the past; *what* questions help you create a better future.
- Asking *what* instead of *why* can help you better understand, name, and manage your emotions.

Let us say you are in a terrible mood after work. Asking "*Why* do I feel this way?" might elicit such unhelpful answers as, "Because I hate my job!" or, "Because I'm not doing good at my work!" Instead, asking, "*What* am I feeling right now?" could lead you to realize you are feeling overwhelmed by the amount of work you have been asked to perform, you have not been getting enough sleep, or it could be as simple as you skipped lunch and are hungry. As we discussed in Outlook, the simple act of labeling your emotions into language—versus simply experiencing them—stops the brain from activating your amygdala, the fight-or-flight command center helping you to stay in control. This knowledge is actionable, and you might decide to grab a snack or commit to an early bedtime.

When You Need to Ask Why

There is one important exception to "What? So What? Now What?" When you are navigating challenges or solving problems externally—with your family, team, and others—asking *why* can be critical. For example, if a member of your team drops the ball on an important, agreed upon responsibility, not exploring why it happened means you risk not understanding their reason and having potential recurrences. If your child does not prepare for an exam, you need to know the reasons to better support her in the future. It is easy to assume the child was just being "lazy" or "irresponsible," but usually there is a deeper reason. A good rule of thumb is the *why* questions generally help us understand events in our environment, and *what* questions help us understand ourselves.

Following are example questions to walk you through the *What? So What? Now What?* Reflection model. We recommend you use this as a guide to customize your personal Reflection process for something that feels natural and authentic.

What?

Asking questions about *what* of the MTM clarifies the facts and establishes context. *What* questions represent the nuts and bolts of what happened in your MTM. (They don't literally have to start with the word "what"; instead they are asking for more information about the situation itself.) This should not be to elicit a play-by-play but rather just enough information to ground yourself in the details. Ask yourself these questions to clarify the facts of your MTM:

- What was the opportunity or challenge in this MTM?
- What happened?
- Who was involved?
- What did I notice (five senses)?
- How did I demonstrate that I care for the people in this MTM?

So What?

So what questions uncover the significance of the insight gained in asking *what*? How did those insights resonate with who you are and what you believe—or constructively challenge your beliefs? Apply relevant past experiences in exploring your MTM. Formulate or adjust important conclusions about what you observed in your current MTM. Remember to consider both a results and relationship perspective! Ask yourself:

- *So what* worked or did not?
- *So what* surprised me?
- *So what* was confirmed?
- *So what* do I still not know?
- *So what* connections can I make between this experience and previous experiences?

Now What?

This is the time to synthesize what you have learned and assess how that can be put into action for future growth. You can do this by asking the following *now what* questions:

- *Now what* does this say about the outlook I should bring to future experiences?
- *Now what* actions will I do differently or the same next time?

- *Now what* is the best way for me to move forward from this experience?
- *Now what* can I do to ensure future success or prevent future failure?
- *Now what* are my goals moving forward from this MTM?

Journal to Reflect

It is important to express your Reflections in some external form—usually written, spoken, or even drawn pictures. Learning and meaning come not only from the *in-the-head* Reflection but from externally expressing those Reflections. We recommend regularly recording Reflections in a private journal.

A journal will provide a readily available outlet to Reflect by expressing your thoughts through writing or pictures, which also helps organize your thinking before possibly sharing those thoughts with others or engaging in another HSC. A Reflection journal will help you also provide documentation of previous Reflections to build upon and track your progress.

A best practice to establish this habit is to predefine a time that works for you to spend 10–15 minutes Reflecting. Most people find the best times are in the morning before the start of a busy day or in the evening before closing out the day. Block your calendar, because without a dedicated time, the busyness of the day will eat up your Reflection.

Reflection Strategy #3: Apply Your Learning to Desired Behavior Change

Following is a checklist of proven practices to convert your Reflection insights into desired behavior change.

✓ **Define the "Fewest, Most Important" Areas for Growth**
   Too many areas will ensure you lose focus and fail at your desired behavior change. You have two choices. The first is to do something

about everything, and the second is to do everything about the most important things. If you choose one or two attainable development goals at a time, you will achieve your desired results more effectively than if you were to tackle a long list of goals at once.

You only have a limited amount of time, energy, and focus. Behavior change is hard, so focusing on one or two important changes is plenty.

✓ Make the Changes Meaningful

Are the behavior changes meaningful and important to you? Changing habits is hard, so identify your motivation or "why." If the "why" for your change is not important enough for you to invest the time and energy required for success, then you likely will not do it. It is important to be honest in this assessment because your motivations are important predictors of success with changing habits or behaviors. Without a strong personal driver, you are set up to fail!

Weight Loss

You have three months until you will be attending your 20th high-school class reunion. Looking in the mirror (your Reflection), you realize that you have put on a few pounds—like 30—since you last walked into your high school. If you have ever been in this pinch, you may have tried a variety of crash diets designed to shed weight quickly. And, if you are like most people, shortly after your high-school reunion, you put the weight back on.

Why? Your "why" for losing weight was short term, like to fit into a particular size or make your old flame jealous for breaking up with you in the 11th grade!

If you want to lose weight and keep it off, have a bigger, stronger "why," like feeling better, lowering blood pressure, staving off diabetes, cutting the risks of heart disease, staying out of the hospital, or being alive to see your grandchildren. Finding more powerful "whys" can help you stick with your goal.

Your "why" in your MTM may be to improve a relationship, eliminate a habitual argument, or advance a team toward project success. Your "why" may closely tie to your MTM goal, as discussed earlier. In Reflection, you can refine that goal based on what you learned during the HSC.

In Shawn Achor's book, *The Happiness Advantage*, he shares the following facts about goals: "Research conclusively shows that those who fail to find high meaning and engagement at work are three times less likely to have life satisfaction and happiness outside of work" (Achor 2018). Meaningful professional goals support your overall well-being and happiness! The same can be said with non-work goals as well!

✓ Look for Small Wins

Small successes are the building blocks of bigger wins, because small changes often have a ripple effect. Research shows that people who work out also begin to eat healthier foods, for example (Ducharme 2019). Define short-term wins to build your confidence for larger and longer-term habit changes. Even if your short-term win is simple, achieving it will build resilience and momentum to try a more challenging change—like moving mountains!

Another advantage of dividing your bigger goals into smaller, more achievable wins is that it allows you to use your brain to your advantage. Studies show that working toward meaningful and achievable goals triggers the brain to release a neurotransmitter called "dopamine" (Monica 2013). This chemical is called the "feel good" neurotransmitter, because it does just that—it makes you feel good.

This dopamine phenomenon is one reason people benefit from to-do lists: the satisfaction of ticking off a small task is linked with a flood of dopamine. Each time your brain gets a whiff of this rewarding neurotransmitter, it will *want* you to repeat the associated behavior. Have you ever created a to-do list that included tasks you would have already done, just so you could check them off? If so, you were taking advantage of this scientific phenomenon!

Go for the Small Win

In their book, *The Progress Principle,* researchers Amabile and Kramer shared that progress does not have to be huge to make a difference in how we perform and stay motivated (Amabile and Kramer 2011). Small wins, breakthroughs, and forward movement are just as powerful as goal completion in fueling our desire to work even harder.

If you are using this concept to motivate team members (or even family members) toward behavior change, or instilling new habits, consider celebrating small wins by acknowledging the tasks completed. Parents of small children understand this when they create chore (or potty!) charts with stickers marking completion. Sometimes a simple, "Well done on ____," to an employee can mean the world and help promote ongoing progress.

If your goal in your MTM is to improve your strained relationship with a family member, then identify one achievable thing you can do in the next two weeks to help. Maybe you can send the person a card to show you are thinking about or appreciate him. Perhaps, it's countering any negative thought about that person with a list of three things you admire about her. These are fully within your control, achievable, and targeted to your meaningful goal: improving your important relationship.

✓ Reinforce Your Change with the Right Social Support

Changing behaviors in isolation requires a good deal of hard work. The bigger your desired change, the more social support you will need. A strong social support network can provide the following two benefits in pursuit of your goal.

Social Support Benefit #1: Accountability. The American Society of Training and Development (ASTD) studied accountability and found that you have a 65 percent chance of completing a goal if you commit to someone (Wissman 2018). And, setting a specific accountability appointment with a person you have committed to increases your chance of success by up to 95 percent.

Speaking your intention creates accountability and solicits support. Find someone who will challenge, engage, and evoke your sense of accomplishment. When accountable to someone or a group, you can more easily get stuff done, because you engage the power of social expectations. When you tell your boss that you will get the proposal done by the end of the week, you are more likely to stick to it and do it. When you tell a client that you will send over a report, you deliver. The expectation alone is enough motivation to commit to and achieve it.

Social Support Benefit #2: Resilience. When obstacles inevitably arise, you will need support to keep your goals in perspective. Your social support system will be there to talk after a setback or bad day, or when you are feeling overwhelmed with too much to do or people being difficult. Support friends, colleagues, and family will help you celebrate successes and encourage you to meet the next challenge, instilling the belief that you can succeed.

✓ Plan for Future Obstacles

You likely are familiar with the obstacles that constantly get in your way of developing new habits and behaviors, particularly when they involve an MTM. Many of the obstacles we continually hear about from our clients include limited time, competing priorities, difficult people, challenging situations, access to information, poor relationships, and so on.

Getting overwhelmed by all your obstacles is not helpful to your belief that you can succeed. Identify the *One Big Thing* that stands in the way of achieving your desired change. Then, proactively develop a plan to mitigate this obstacle. By doing so, you will keep moving forward when difficulty arises (Dalio 2019).

Answering the following questions will help you work around predictable barriers. Ask yourself:

- What is the *one big thing* that will stand in the way of accomplishing my behavior change?
- What can I do to stop this *one big thing* from obscuring my success?

Remember that you will not be perfect. In any behavior change, leaning on old, unproductive habits is natural. During a setback, you may feel disappointed and frustrated. One of the greatest barriers to your own change efforts is failing to acknowledge that setbacks are part of the growth process.

Bill's One Big Thing

In 1935, a failing Wall Street worker named Bill Wilson had grown tired of the career setbacks caused by his ongoing drinking. With Reflection on his past, he realized that the reason he never got his law degree was alcohol: he failed to pick up his diploma, because he was too drunk to attend graduation. His marriage suffered, and he was institutionalized for alcoholism.

He committed to quit drinking but found himself very tempted. Desperate to stay sober, he sought someone who might understand his obsession. He called several ministers, asking if they knew any alcoholics. Those calls led him to a man named Dr. Bob Smith. Smith had barely completed medical school because of his own drinking, and while he opened a clinic and married, his life was held together by a thread.

Dr. Bob committed to give Bill 15 minutes. They spoke for six hours. That night in 1935, Wilson and Smith started what is known today as Alcoholics Anonymous, a community brought together by one common goal: to stay sober. Hallmarks of this group include social support (meetings across the globe), accountability (sponsor and fellow members), and planning for obstacles (following the 12 steps as outlined in *The Big Book of Alcoholics Anonymous*).

Since its inception, other groups have cropped up around the globe applying some of the same methodology to help people struggling with addiction to drugs, gambling, sex, food, and so on.

Bill identified his big thing, and through social support, was able to achieve even greater goals than he had previously set (History of Alcoholics Anonymous 2020).

Regardless of the behavior change you are making, some of these same principles can apply.

Too often, people view setbacks as failure, feeding disappointment and loss of the drive for those improvements. Growth and development require "grit." In Jon Acuff's book, *Do Over*, he describes grit: "Grit is being stubborn in the face of fear. Grit is the first time you try something, and it is the thousandth time too. Grit is believing in *can* when *cannot* is loud. We think grit is grimaces and grinding it out and wiping sweat of your brow as you save the day! We think it will feel great. Here is the truth about grit:

Grit makes you feel like throwing up.
Grit feels like crying. A lot.
Grit feels like losing sleep" (Acuff 2015)."

This is why meaningful, small wins; social support; and planning for obstacles are crucial. They build grit during the setbacks that come with growth. Setbacks need not undermine your self-confidence. If you lapse back to an old behavior, Reflect on the "What? So What? Now What?" of the setback and leverage your insights to plan how to get back on track. If you were to take a wrong turn on the way to a vacation destination, you would not turn around and go home, right? You would figure out the quickest way to get back on your route. Adjusting to setbacks is a natural and crucial part of your development journey and will build resilience for your next MTM.

Successful navigation of the SOAR cycle has never been more important than in today's fast-moving, complex environment. The U.S. Army War College coined the term VUCA to describe the volatility, uncertainty, complexity, and ambiguity of the world after the Cold War. It has also been used to describe the recent business climate as technology, political pressure, and ever-changing market needs require rapid and ongoing adaptation. Our day-to-day lives rely more than ever on our abilities to demonstrate self-leadership through mindfulness, emotional awareness (self and others), social skills, and learning agility to survive and thrive. Research confirms what our intuition already knows: the most successful people are adept at continually adapting to meet the needs of their changing environments.

Back to our sailing analogy, having a strong boat is important, but it might not be as crucial as having a self-aware and skilled crew that can nimbly adjust to the wind, current, seas, and other obstacles that arise. In order to SOAR to your destination, each SOAR concept must be activated dynamically in real time—with Reflection being key to learn from and adjust after each leg of the journey. A crew that is motivated not to sink will gladly take on this challenge.

Imagine standing on a scale after a month of changing your diet. You worked hard the previous month to eat better, get active, and cut back on your portion size. But the only way to know if it paid off is to step on the scale. You hope to see that your weight declined, at least a little. The scale is an objective, honest form of feedback. Reflection on that feedback—and the new planning that comes from it—allows you to adjust or cement your habits for ongoing progress.

Similarly, Reflection forces you to look honestly at your strengths and areas that require improvement, gaining insights to test on future experiences. Reflection is the primary way to examine your Self (and how others see you), understand and improve your Outlook, and adjust your Action for ongoing progress in advancing your MTM. Like a master painter who steps back after focusing on a particular area of a painting, Reflection allows you to assess your recent actions against the big picture—providing perspective to adjust or move in the same direction, if all is well.

Reflection includes the important steps of asking for feedback, answering "*What? So What? Now What?*," and setting the right goals for effective behavior change before your next critical moment. These are instrumental to your evolution. If you want to Get It Right When It Matters Most, Reflection will design your continuous improvement. Reflection tells you what to repeat and what to change.

Reflection: Self-Assessment and Review

Now that you have finished reading the *Reflection phase*, read the following statements (Table 12.1) and assess your current proficiency using the following scale:

Table 12.1 Reflection: Self-assessment and review

5—Strongly agree

4—Agree

3—Neither agree nor disagree

2—Disagree

1—Strongly agree

1. I know how to reflect to learn from my experiences.	5	4	3	2	1
2. I actively seek feedback for continuous learning.	5	4	3	2	1
3. I am able to listen to constructive feedback without being defensive.	5	4	3	2	1
4. I actively set development goals for ongoing improvement.	5	4	3	2	1
5. I share my goals with people who I trust and will support my progress.	5	4	3	2	1
6. I regularly practice new skills or new approaches to continually develop important skills.	5	4	3	2	1
7. I understand how to create development goals that are meaningful and achievable.	5	4	3	2	1
8. I know how to create a supportive social network for me successfully learn and grow.	5	4	3	2	1
9. I create clear plans for overcoming recurring obstacles for my learning and development.	5	4	3	2	1

Consider making an action plan for any scores that fall lower than a 4 on these statements. Where scores fall at the 3 or below represent where you are most vulnerable to *getting it wrong* in your MTMs.

CHAPTER 13

Pulling It All Together for Productive Moments That Matter

To learn and not to do is really not to learn. To know and not to do is really not to know.

—Stephen R. Covey

At this point, some of you might relate to this classic joke: A turtle was crossing the road when he got mugged by two snails. When the police showed up, they asked him what happened. The shaken turtle replies, "I don't know. It all happened so fast."

Perhaps you read this book in a few days, and it felt like sipping from a fire hose: too much to take in so quickly! And that might lead you to believe that the SOAR model and its learning points cannot possibly be processed and applied.

It takes time to master new skills, but these principles work.

If you were a sailboat captain trying to SOAR to your destination, we have given you a safe place to practice navigating your boat (Self), testing your systems and sails (Outlook), and planning your route—including how to steer around the cargo ships and storms ahead (Action). Finally, you have planned your next Actions by learning through what you encountered (Reflection).

Read on to see how Sheila (not her real name) applied these truths in action. Here's how she told it to us.

Sheila's High-Stakes Conversation (HSC)

After a ton of work and vetting with key stakeholders, Sheila and her team were excited to launch an initiative. So, Sheila sent an email officially informing the executive team about the launch of a new company-wide system designed to improve tracking of project progress while enhancing development of current and future project managers.

Minutes after sending the announcement, Sheila received an email from Alex, an executive who had also copied the executive team, including the chief executive officer (CEO) and Sheila's manager, stating that his division would "not be participating in this new initiative" because it would not meet "their unique needs."

"What the *&%$?!*" Sheila thought as she sat boiling at her desk. "I can't believe he did this—*again!*"

Obviously, this was not Sheila's first rodeo with Alex—who had a habit of verbalizing he was not on board only *after* witnessing the entire process unfold (while being kept in the loop the whole time). And it certainly was not the first time he had copied the entire executive team about his disapproval of a project Sheila's area had launched.

What really irked Sheila this time was that she and her team deliberately had worked very closely with Alex's division. Members of Alex's team were at every meeting along the way, and they indicated that they understood and agreed with the direction Sheila laid out.

"Thanks, Alex," Sheila said shaking her head. What she meant was, thanks *to* Alex, a big, fat MTM got shoved down her throat!

Why was this an MTM for Sheila? Delivering this new process was *important* to her team's success for the quarter. Her boss made it her top goal. The situation was also *complex*, because if there were a way to prevent Alex from acting out like he had just done or to get him on board, Shelia certainly did not know it. And this event was *relational*, as Alex was an influential executive who had just thrown her new process under the bus. *Yup*, Sheila knew, *this is an MTM, like it or not*.

Sheila needed to engage Alex in an HSC.

Sheila Prepares Her Self and Outlook for the High-Stakes Conversation

With each footstep on her way to Alex's office, Sheila noticed she almost stomped on the floor. She walked into the restroom to slow herself down.

"I'm so angry at him," she said to her reflection in the mirror. Underneath her anger, she also felt a swell of anxiety. "If Alex doesn't get on board, I will have failed to achieve this strategic goal," she acknowledged to herself. Thinking of her ARC, her Competence was threatened. Her Outlook was clouded by her own biases, thinking he was being difficult because his character was flawed.

That is when Shelia stopped. She remembered her own strengths—as a high Achiever according to the Strengths 2.0 assessment she took. She also remembered her value of Collaboration, which drove her to want to try to work with Alex. She recognized that she may have biases at play—and that Alex may have other strengths, such as Communication, which she could tap into.

She paused and then took a few deep breaths, thinking, *inhale 1...2...3...4*, followed by an extended *exhale 1...2...3...4...5...6*. After taking three or four deliberate breaths, Sheila felt more balanced and relaxed. Sheila labeled her feelings as angry and anxious about having to engage Alex in this HSC. She acknowledged her pressure to reestablish an effective partnership with Alex (which could lead to a relational threat).

As Sheila turned the last corner before reaching Alex's door, she reminded herself that her long-term goal was to *develop a more productive, trusting relationship with Alex*. In her head, Sheila named her intentions for this particular meeting: *to make sure Alex feels heard about his concerns and comes to mutually beneficial agreements for moving forward.*

Sheila's High-Stakes Conversation
Step #1: Align on the Issue

Sheila knocked on the door frame, and Alex motioned for her to come in.

"Hey, Sheila," Alex said cheerfully. "Have a seat. I'm guessing this is about my response to your new process."

"Hi, Alex," Sheila responded trying to contain her nerves. "You must be a mind reader," she said with a small laugh.

After clearing her throat, Sheila began speaking again. "Specifically, I would love to hear your concerns about what my team launched. And then I hope to find a way to work together so we can salvage this situation and hopefully work better together down the road."

Alex nodded. "Sure, I'd be happy to outline in more detail my main concern. And I'd really value being able to get the kind of support we need in my division."

Alex then began listing off his concerns while Sheila took careful notes. Alex said he wasn't convinced that this new process would address his project managers' unique needs. Then, he expressed frustration that he hadn't been engaged earlier in the process. He said that most corporate projects didn't ask for feedback until there was a draft proposal, and then it was too late for him to have any real influence. So, he felt that he had little choice but to call it out when the message about the kick-off was sent to the executive team.

"I'm not saying that this oversight was deliberate or personal," Alex continued. "And again, your area isn't the only one that tries to launch programs without talking to all of the stakeholders in depth." Sheila perceived his lack of input earlier in the process as a primary issue with this new process. Sheila quickly confirmed this assumption by paraphrasing that she felt Alex's lack of input earlier in the process was the primary issue. Alex responded that this was his primary issue.

Now that Sheila had clarity on Alex's concerns, she tried to better understand Alex's perspectives around this issue.

Sheila's High-Stakes Conversation Step #2: Explore Perspectives

In her past encounters with Alex, Sheila had tried to defend her team and challenge Alex's position. Let us just say that approach did not work out well. This time, Sheila took note of her emotions of frustration and defensiveness. Then she inhaled and recommitted to her personal best intention to *make sure Alex feels heard about his concerns and comes to mutually beneficial agreements for moving forward.*

Sheila asked Quality Questions to better understand Alex's take on the "not being engaged earlier" issue of the design process. Sheila asked Alex three questions to get a better handle on his perspective:

- What about the way we have implemented this and previous projects could be improved from your perspective?
- What else should I understand about your perspectives about how to effectively engage your division?

- How does this specific new project management process miss the mark for your division?

By asking these questions and deliberately listening, Sheila gained awareness about his concerns. She learned that Alex wanted to be included earlier in the design of initiatives impacting his division. She also learned that when she or her team came to him with a written draft for feedback, it made him feel defensive, because he felt it was too late to truly influence or provide feedback. Finally, she learned that Alex had emotions! Seeing the proposal late in the game made him frustrated, because he felt input would be useless.

Sheila had no clue these were Alex's concerns. Most other executives wanted no part of the early design process. Instead, they sent representatives from their team to do this work and provide feedback to a developed draft. But Sheila learned that Alex didn't just want her to work with his team; he wanted to be personally involved. Sheila did not realize that until her HSC, and she would've never known this had she not asked Quality Questions.

Balance Asking for the Other's Perspective and Sharing Her Own

"I am so glad I asked you about this, Alex," Sheila said, genuinely excited. "I can see where you thought that I wasn't interested in your opinions. In reality, I know how busy you and the other executives are. My not reaching out to you was my false belief that, like your peers, you wouldn't want to talk with me early in the process. I intended to respect your time. Now that I know your desire, I can make this an easy fix moving forward!"

Sheila received this feedback with gratitude. Not only would she love his feedback earlier in the design, but this one change would give her a better way to partner and build a positive relationship with Alex in the future.

Sheila's High-Stakes Conversation
Step #3: Generate Forward-Focused Solutions

Armed with the information Alex just shared, Sheila immediately asked solution-focused Quality Questions. Here is what she asked:

- How do you need me to engage you prior to the launch of future projects?
- How would you like to be included in the design process of new projects?
- What is your right level of involvement and influence moving forward?
- How would you like for us to include members of your division in the future design of new projects?
- What can I do differently in communicating with you, so that you feel adequately informed?

"Great questions," Alex replied, eager to have a chance to lay out his expectations. "Well, here's what I would like…"

By the time Alex finished, Sheila learned that Alex wanted input on the scope and early project design but not the day-to-day design. He wanted ongoing progress updates prior to Sheila addressing the executives for feedback and final approval. He offered to meet with her weekly to discuss ongoing updates and provide feedback. He also shared that anytime her department was going to share a broad communication either to Alex's peers or the organization that she should give him a heads up.

"You know," Alex concluded, "If you want my full support, I want to see any communication you plan to send to my peers so I can adjust the message to include how you're working directly with my division. I'm not trying to micromanage your work. But if you have my support, you'll get the support from my peers."

Sheila knew that making these "concessions" to Alex would add more time, but she also knew the huge benefit of an executive's buy-in and feedback would be well worth the investment.

Sheila and Alex agreed that Alex would not receive any broad communications without her getting his feedback. Sheila asked additional follow-up questions about Alex's preferred way for her to reach out to him and Alex's receptivity to face-to-face meetings for more complex communications.

Sheila shared her perspective about needing Alex to be responsive, so this agreement would not delay her department's timelines. Alex understood and said he would make sure he and his team were responsive.

Sheila's High-Stakes Conversation
Step #4: Take Shared Action

Having come this far, Sheila would not leave this HSC without explicit agreements on how to move forward in more aligned, coordinated, and productive ways. Sheila asked Alex one simple question: *"What agreements can we make about next steps?"*

Alex gave multiple fair and straightforward suggestions. Based on his input, they made the following agreements for coordinated action moving forward:

- Alex would not receive formal communication about projects that impacted his division without first engaging him directly.
- Sheila would schedule regular meetings to provide input when his team began to design any project impacting his division.
- Alex gave the name of someone on his communications team to provide feedback about future messages to ensure inclusiveness of his division's unique needs.

Regarding the project Sheila just launched and communicated, the two agreed to move forward with the new project management process, as most of Alex's concerns were about having earlier influence and inclusion in projects that impacted his division. Sheila felt this HSC had moved forward their relationship, as they had gained mutual respect. By clarifying the issue, exploring perspectives, creating solutions, and agreeing on shared action, they had built a solid foundation for future success.

Note: The authors do not wish to belabor Sheila's story by pointing out how she applied every learning point in this book. Instead, Sheila's story focuses on the apex of the SOAR model: the HSC. As Sheila demonstrated, applying the right Action to an MTM can make all the difference in the outcome.

Reflecting on It All

As Sheila walked away from her meeting with Alex—and throughout the next several months as they cemented their growing relationship and process—she engaged in ongoing Reflection about their MTM. She asked him for regular feedback on how she was doing in applying his ideas. She contemplated the significance of their conversations, realizing they could gain her greater access to an executive to better understand her senior leaders' goals and needs. She celebrated their mutual small successes along the way—such as when Alex's communications person made valuable edits to her proposed upcoming email.

Does Sheila's story make the process look easy? Hopefully you can see how the major elements of SOAR cycle work together to break down MTMs into simpler actions.

Sheila's success in her MTM started with checking her emotions and desire to be right at any cost. She worked through her anger and reminded herself of her intentions. Then she played the role of a journalist, asking the right questions to get detailed information from Alex. Finally, her conversation demonstrated willingness to adjust to satisfy Alex, developing their relationship while securing his approval for her project's launch.

Think of a current MTM you are facing. Review the elements of Sheila's story that relate to yours. Look at the highlights of Sheila's process, and visualize having a similar conversation. Realize that the same process can work for you. You have all the tools you need. Now you just need practice!

CHAPTER 14

"But It Didn't Work!" Read On...

You may encounter many defeats, but you must not be defeated.
—Maya Angelou

If you have read and applied what we have shared so far, you are ahead of the average person when it comes to *Getting It Right When It Matters Most.* As a review, you have learned about:

- *Self.* The whole of you that comes to every situation you face.
- *Outlook.* The lens by which you interpret people and events.
- *Action.* The steps you take to navigate your MTM's High-Stakes Conversation (HSC).
- *Reflection.* The self-assessment of what worked, what didn't work and what to do differently next time.

According to experts on the circulatory system, it takes about one minute for the heart to pump blood out of the left ventricle and carry it through the whole body before returning it to the right atrium, where the process starts again ("How Long Does it Take For Blood To Flow Round The Body?" 2020). Similarly, SOAR is a never-ending cycle that lasts as long as we live. (Just do not expect our model to be finished cycling in a minute!) While our hearts bring in oxygen-poor blood and pump out oxygen-rich blood, implementing SOAR converts ineffective habits and refreshes them by updating your Self, Outlook, Action, and Reflection— especially during your important, complex, and relational MTMs. Each time you Reflect on what you have learned, you can update your best version of Self for your next MTM.

Am I Doing It Wrong? It Did Not Work!

At times, you will do the very best you can to achieve a successful outcome for your MTM, and for whatever reason, it does not go the way you planned. When that happens, your best tool is to invest in Reflection. Answer honest questions about yourself and your approach:

- Did I do enough background work to understand my Best Self—and blind spots that could bring out my Worst Self?
- Did I manage my emotions as I entered the MTM?
- Did I check my biases at the door to keep any desire to "be right" at bay?
- Did I detail my best intention for the MTM?
- Did I prepare for my HSC, choosing open-ended Quality Questions that had no accusatory tone or intentions?
- Did I balance between getting the other person's perspective as well as stating my own?
- Did I work with the other person to generate solutions and take shared Action?

If you did all these things and still did not achieve your desired results, reflection may uncover where things started falling apart. List what you did well. Then list the things you want to do differently next time.

If after Reflection you still find no room for improvement, the problem does not likely fall at your end. Not everyone wants to change, get along, be agreeable, or find solutions. While some people seem programmed to resist your best efforts, fortunately, these people are in the minority.

Psychology Professor Gladin

In graduate school, Scott's professor shared insight from his lifetime of counseling and teaching others: *"You can't save everyone. Not everyone wants to be saved."*

The same holds true if you substitute the word *save* for *change, help,* or *empower.* Some will not choose to cooperate, usually because of misaligned perspectives rooted in differing values or goals. Too often in these cases, the issue can become overly personal, which sometimes makes it impossible to recover any true collaboration.

If It Did Not Work, Why Should I Keep Trying?

In a perfect world, we could all circumvent free will by using Jedi mind tricks on people we wished to change. We could just wave a hand and say, "This person makes perfect sense. I should listen to him."

But alas, free will cannot be easily manipulated. You will face MTMs where you will do everything within your power, yet the other person will not see things your way or even try to work with you. What then?

Following are reasons why you should practice SOAR and the numerous tips in this book even if you do not see instant results.

Your Well-Being Is as Important as Your Results

In the Self phase, we recommended that you increase your self-awareness through various personality assessments and ask others for feedback about the parts of your personality you cannot see with ease. Knowing your strengths and weaknesses, aligning yourself with your core values, activating Your Best Self, and practicing self-care helps maintain your emotional well-being.

People with higher well-being have a greater resilience to stress, deeper relationships, higher self-esteem, and more energy ("How to Build Good Emotional Health" 2020). Pharmaceutical companies seem to have a pill for everything. But by prioritizing Your Best Self to show up in how you approach others, you do more than any one pill can accomplish. And, you might just avoid a doctor visit, co-pay, or prescription.

Practice Makes Permanent

Remember when you learned to ride a bike? You looked in front of you, steadied the handlebars, leaned and steered into turns, avoided obstacles, figured out how to stop, and kept pedaling all at the same time. Once you learned the basics, you could ride and steer with no hands! It did not happen instantly. But the more you practiced, the easier and more natural it became.

While not every MTM will come to a satisfactory conclusion, the skills you practice as you strive for mastery will equip you to make other MTMs SOAR! Over time, you will use these new skills so often and with such fluency, you will not remember a time when you had to think about them consciously. And that is the goal: upgrading your new operating system to something that works.

Preventing Faux Pas

Only a sociopath wakes up in the morning wondering how to make someone else's life miserable. The vast majority of us do the best we can, and treat others the best we can, throughout each day. But, we still make mistakes.

Sometimes it isn't the words we say but our faces that betray our negative emotions. We spent much of this book sharing tips to regain emotional control when triggered. Some may struggle with implementing parts of the Action phase, but everyone can benefit from pausing, breathing, and labeling their emotions. Practicing these simple tips can prevent faux pas, saying or doing the wrong thing at the wrong time.

Your Reputation Is Built One MTM at a Time

Even when an MTM does not work as planned, wins often come later. Think in terms of your reputation. Aristotle said, "We are what we repeatedly do." Every leader we know wants to be seen as self-aware, level-headed, fair, and effective. But how do leaders earn that reputation? They are habitually self-aware, level-headed, fair, and effective. That does not mean they win arguments, are right 100 percent of the time, or have the loudest voices in the room.

One of the authors had a colleague, Nabila, who had been assigned goals and responsibilities that overlapped his own. The two of them met multiple times and could not find common ground to move forward. Both parties left these interactions feeling frustrated, neither having received his or her desired outcome.

Fast-forward five years when both worked at different companies. Nabila reached out to the author to see if he would be interested in partnering with her and her team with some really interesting and important work with developing their companies' leaders. Why did Nabila reach out in a way that benefited the author professionally and financially? Because the author had become known for handling differences in a constructive way.

When you approach an MTM with a "growth mindset" that tells you that you can be effective, you can bring Your Best Self forward, you can better understand the other person's perspective, there is a good chance that you will achieve those things. But even when you do not, you will have further cemented your reputation as one who is self-aware, level-headed, fair, and effective.

The Platinum Rules

Not every moment in life matters as much as your most important, complex, and relational ones. You have heard that "even a broken clock is right twice a day." When it comes to your MTMs, such a low accuracy rate would mean you would experience chronic failure when things mattered most.

The Platinum Rule states that *we should do unto others the way they want us to do unto them.* So how do you accomplish that? You interact with others…

- …as a potential ally instead of adversary
- …with Your Best Self coming out instead of Your Worst Self
- …without letting your biases cloud your lens
- …with genuine curiosity so you can learn others' perspectives
- …using questions and not just declarations
- …with a desire to collaborate to achieve results

And everybody wins—either by advancing their MTM or learning valuable lessons for *Getting It Right When It Matters Most.*

References

2020. *Reflective Practice Guide*. CIPD. https://cipd.co.uk/Images/reflective-practice-guide_tcm18-12524.pdf (accessed April 7, 2020).

Achor, S. 2018. *The Happiness Advantage: How a Positive Brain Fuels Success in Work and Life*. New York, NY: Currency.

Acuff, J. 2015. *Do over: Rescue Monday, Reinvent Your Work, and Never Get Stuck*. New York, NY: Portfolio/Penguin.

Amabile, T., and S. Kramer. 2011. *The Progress Principle: Using Small Wins to Ignite Joy, Engagement, and Creativity at Work*. Boston, MA: Harvard Business Review Press.

"America's #1 Health Problem." 2017. *The American Institute of Stress*. https://stress.org/americas-1-health-problem (accessed January 4, 2017).

Anseel, F., F. Lievens, and E. Schollaert. 2009. "Reflection as a Strategy to Enhance Task Performance after Feedback." *Organizational Behavior and Human Decision Processes* 110, no. 1, 23–35. doi:10.1016/j.obhdp.2009.05.003

Baumeister, R.F., E. Bratslavsky, C. Finkenauer, and K.D. Vohs. 2001. "Bad Is Stronger than Good." *Review of General Psychology* 5, no. 4, 323–370. doi:10.1037/1089-2680.5.4.323

Brothers, C. 2005. *Language and the Pursuit of Happiness: a New Foundation for Designing Your Life, Your Relationships & Your Results*. Naples, FL: New Possibilities Press.

Bruce, A. 2001. *Leaders - Start to Finish: a Road Map for Developing and Training Leaders at All Levels*. Alexandria, VA: American Society for Training and Development.

Buckingham, M., and D.O. Clifton. 2005. *Now, Discover Your Strengths: How to Develop Your Talents and Those of the People You Manage*. London, UK: Pocket Books.

Cappucci, M. 2019. "Flight Reaches 801 Mph as a Furious Jet Stream Packs Record-Breaking Speeds." *The Washington Post*. WP Company. https://washingtonpost.com/weather/2019/02/19/flight-reaches-mph-furious-jet-stream-packs-record-breaking-speeds (accessed February 19, 2019).

Carbonara, S., and R. Grimes. 2020. Personal.

Carbonara, S., and S. Mueller. 2019. Personal.

Carbonara, S., and T. Ryan. 2020. Interview with Tim Ryan. Personal.

Carbonara, S. 2013. *Manager's Guide to Employee Engagement*. New York, NY: McGraw-Hill.

Chism, M. 2011. *Stop Workplace Drama: Run Your Office with No Complaints, No Excuses, and No Regrets*. Hoboken, NJ: Wiley.

Chism, M. 2016. *No-Drama Leadership: How Enlightened Leaders Transform Culture in the Workplace*. New York, NY: Routledge.

Covey, S.R. 2004. *Seven Habits of Highly Effective People*. London, UK: Simon and Schuster.

Csikszentmihalyi, M. 2009. *Flow: The Psychology of Optimal Experience*. New York, NY: Harper Row.

Dalio, R. 2019. *Principles for Success*. New York, NY: Avid Reader Press / Simon & Schuster.

Danziger, S., J. Levav, and L. Avnaim-Pesso. 2011. "Extraneous Factors in Judicial Decisions." *PNAS*. National Academy of Sciences. https://pnas.org/content/108/17/6889.full (accessed April 26, 2011).

Ducharme, J. 2019. "Exercising Might Help You Make Healthier Food Choices, Study Says." *Time*. https://time.com/5517552/exercise-eat-healthier/ (accessed February 6, 2019).

Duhigg, C. 2016. "What Google Learned From Its Quest to Build the Perfect Team." *The New York Times*. https://nytimes.com/2016/02/28/magazine/what-google-learned-from-its-quest-to-build-the-perfect-team.html (accessed February 25, 2016).

Dweck, C.S. 2017. *Mindset*. London, UK: Robinson, an imprint of Constable & Robinson Ltd.

Eisenberger, N.I. 2003. "Does Rejection Hurt? An FMRI Study of Social Exclusion." *Science* 302, no. 5643, 290–292. doi:10.1126/science.1089134

Eliot, T.S. 1961. *The Dry Salvages*. London, UK: Faber and Faber.

Epstein, J., and S. Mannes. 2016. "'Gruesome' Evidence, Science, and Rule 403." *The National Judicial College*, https://judges.org/gruesome-evidence-science-and-rule-403/ (accessed October 24, 2016).

Gallup, Inc. 2020. "Gallup Daily: U.S. Employee Engagement." *Gallup.com*. Gallup, https://news.gallup.com/poll/180404/gallup-daily-employee-engagement.aspx (accessed March 12, 2020).

Goldsmith, M. 2017. *What Got You Here Won't Get You There*. New York, NY: Hachette Book Group.

The Godfather. 2004. Film. Place of publication not identified: Paramount.

Hanson, R. 2016. "Overcoming the Negativity Bias." *Dr. Rick Hanson*, https://rickhanson.net/overcoming-negativity-bias/ (accessed November 30, 2016).

Hedges, K. 2012. "Do You Feel Lonely As A Leader? Study Says You're Not Alone." *Forbes*, Forbes Magazine. https://forbes.com/sites/work-in-progress/2012/02/23/if-mark-zuckerberg-is-lonely-heres-my-solution/#42bca037c43a (accessed March 6, 2012).

"History of Alcoholics Anonymous." 2020. *Wikipedia*. Wikimedia Foundation, https://en.wikipedia.org/wiki/History_of_Alcoholics_Anonymous (accessed March 22, 2020).

Hogan, B. 2019. "Steve Chapman: Memo to the next President: Hit the Hay." *Omaha.com*. Omaha World Herald, https://omaha.com/opinion/steve-chapman-memo-to-the-next-president-hit-the-hay/article_523256df-9282-5ecb-a150-1cb196657d3f.html (accessed June 25, 2019).

"How Long Does It Take For Blood To Flow Round The Body?" 2011. *LBC*. https://lbc.co.uk/radio/special-shows/the-mystery-hour/human-body/how-long-does-it-take-for-blood-to-flow-round-the/ (accessed November 11, 2011).

"How to Build Good Emotional Health." 2020. *Healthline*. https://healthline.com/health/emotional-health#improvement (accessed April 9, 2020).

"How to Develop Self-Awareness." 2017. *Leadership*. Cape Media House. http://leadershiponline.co.za/articles/self-awareness-22548.html (accessed August 7, 2017).

Jaret, P., S. Hickman, C. Willard, W. Kuyken, J. Hunter, O.J. Sofer, G. Bullock, and K.M. Newman. 2020. "What Is Mindfulness?" *Mindful*. https://mindful.org/what-is-mindfulness/(accessed February 11, 2020).

Kahneman, D. 2015. *Thinking, Fast and Slow*. New York, NY: Farrar, Straus and Giroux.

Khazan, I.Z. 2013. *The Clinical Handbook of Biofeedback: a Step-by-Step Guide for Training and Practice with Mindfulness*. Chichester, West Sussex, UK: Wiley-Blackwell.

Lieberman, M. 2015. *Social - Why Our Brains Are Wired to Connect*. Oxford, UK: Oxford University Press.

Living, O. 2017. "The Science Behind Why Naming Our Feelings Makes Us Happier." *HuffPost*, https://huffpost.com/entry/the-science-behind-why-na_b_7174164 (accessed December 7, 2017).

Luft, J., and H. Ingham. 1955. "The Johari Window, a Graphic Model of Interpersonal Awareness." *Proceedings of the Western Training Laboratory in Group Development*.

Ma-Kellams, C., and J. Lerner. 2016. "Trust Your Gut or Think Carefully? Examining Whether an Intuitive, Versus a Systematic, Mode of Thought Produces Greater Empathic Accuracy." *SSRN Electronic Journal* 111, no. 5, 674. doi:10.2139/ssrn.2782596

Maister, D.H., C.H. Green, and R.M. Galford. 2002. *The Trusted Advisor*. London, UK: Simon & Schuster.

McQuaid, M. 2014. "Ten Reasons to Focus on Your Strengths." *Psychology Today*. Sussex Publishers. https://psychologytoday.com/us/blog/functioning-flourishing/201411/ten-reasons-focus-your-strengths (accessed November 11, 2014).

Mehrabian, A. 1981. *Silent Messages: Implicit Communication of Emotions.* Independence, KY: Wadsworth Pub. Co.

Mischel, W., and E.B. Ebbesen. 1970. "Attention in Delay of Gratification." *Journal of Personality and Social Psychology* 16, no. 2, 329–437. doi:10.1037/ h0029815

Monica, M. 2013. *The Entrepreneurial Instinct: How Everyone Has the Innate Ability to Start a Successful Small Business.* New York, NY: McGraw-Hill.

Philippot, P., G. Chapelle, and S. Blairy. 2002. "Respiratory Feedback in the Generation of Emotion." *Cognition & Emotion* 16, no. 5, 605–627. doi:10.1080/02699930143000392

Rath, T., and D.O. Clifton. 2020. "The Big Impact of Small Interactions." *Gallup.com*, February 6. https://news.gallup.com/businessjournal/12916/ big-impact-small-interactions.aspx

Rolfe, G., D. Freshwater, and M. Jasper. 2001. *Critical Reflection for Nursing and the Helping Professions: a User's Guide.* Houndmills, Basingstoke, Hampshire: Palgrave.

Ryan, R.M., and E.L. Deci. 2000. "Self-Determination Theory and the Facilitation of Intrinsic Motivation, Social Development, and Well-Being." *American Psychologist* 55, no. 1, 68–78. doi:10.1037/0003-066x.55.1.68

Saporito, T.J. 2014. "It's Time to Acknowledge CEO Loneliness." *Harvard Business Review.* https://hbr.org/2012/02/its-time-to-acknowledge-ceo-lo (accessed July 23, 2014).

"The Science Behind Meditation." 2020. *Headspace.* https://headspace.com/ science (accessed April 7, 2020).

Siegel, D. 2004. "Dan Siegel: Name It to Tame It." https://youtube.com/ watch?v=ZcDLzppD4Jc

Staff, Edited by Editorial. 2020. "Are You Self-Medicating & Masking Symptoms of Mental Illness?" *American Addiction Centers.* https:// americanaddictioncenters.org/adult-addiction-treatment-programs/self-medicating (accessed April 7, 2020).

"State of Employee Engagement." 2020. *Officevibe.* https://officevibe.com/state-employee-engagement. (accessed April 10, 2020).

Steckl, C. 2020. "Two Keys to Self-Esteem." *Two Keys to Self-Esteem - Self Esteem.* http://wyomentalhealth.org/poc/view_doc.php?type=doc&id=50891 &cn=96 (accessed April 7, 2020).

Williams, J.M.G., and J. Kabat-Zinn. 2011. "Mindfulness: Diverse Perspectives on Its Meaning, Origins, and Multiple Applications at the Intersection of Science and Dharma." *Contemporary Buddhism* 12, no. 1, 1–18. doi:10.1080 /14639947.2011.564811

Williamson, A.M. 2000. "Moderate Sleep Deprivation Produces Impairments in Cognitive and Motor Performance Equivalent to Legally Prescribed Levels of Alcohol Intoxication." *Occupational and Environmental Medicine* 57, no. 10, 649–655. doi:10.1136/oem.57.10.649

Wilson, T.D. 2004. *Strangers to Ourselves: Discovering the Adaptive Unconscious.* Cambridge, MA: Belknap.

Winerman, L. 2005. "The Mind's Mirror A New Type of Neuron--Called a Mirror Neuron--Could Help Explain How We Learn through Mimicry and Why We Empathize with Others." *Monitor on Psychology.* American Psychological Association. https://apa.org/monitor/oct05/mirror (accessed October, 2005)

Wissman, B. 2018. "An Accountability Partner Makes You Vastly More Apt to Succeed." *Entrepreneur.* https://entrepreneur.com/article/310062 (accessed March 20, 2018).

About the Authors

Tony Gambill, MS, HR Development, SPHR, brings more than 20 years of executive experience in coaching, talent development, and delivering impactful leadership solutions within global for-profit, non-profit, technical, research, government, and higher educational industries. Before starting ClearView Leadership Consulting, Tony was the Vice President of Organizational Development and Learning at RTI International for nine years; prior to that, he served as the director of leadership development services at Virginia Tech and Conservation International.

Tony provides executive coaching, leadership development and organizational effectiveness consulting for global for-profit and non-profit organizations. Tony provides strategic perspectives combined with practical expertise building knowledge, skills, and processes for leadership excellence and career growth. Tony has an active following on LinkedIn and is a contributor for Forbes leadership where he regularly writes content on leadership and talent development. Connect with Tony at www.ClearViewLeaders.com, LinkedIn or on Forbes leadership.

Scott Carbonara, MA, Psychology and Communications, is CEO of Spiritus Communications, a consulting company specializing in equipping leaders and elevating lives. Scott is known as the Leadership Therapist for his unique background, from serving as an award-winning family crisis counselor for at-risk families to highly regarded executive chief of staff for Healthcare Services Corporation, the parent company of BlueCross BlueShield of Texas, Illinois, Oklahoma, Montana, and New Mexico, where he guided 13,000+ employees through extensive changes and mergers and solved complex issues that converted a dismal attrition rate of 38 percent to a phenomenal 6.5 percent while drastically improving customer loyalty scores and saving millions of dollars.

Today, Scott is an award-winning international speaker, consultant, and author of several leadership books: *Manager's Guide to Employee Engagement* (McGraw Hill) and *Go Positive, Lead to Engage (coauthored training program, Pfeiffer/John Wiley and Sons)*. Scott has spoken for international conferences. Connect with Scott at www.LeadToEngage. com or on LinkedIn.

Index

OTHER TITLES IN THE BUSINESS CAREER DEVELOPMENT COLLECTION

Vilma Barr, Consultant, Editor

- *Finding Your Career Niche* by Anne S. Klein
- *Shaping Your Future* by Rita Rocker-Craft
- *The Trust Factor* by Russell von Frank
- *Financing New Ventures* by Geoffrey Gregson
- *Strategic Bootstrapping* by Matthew W. Rutherford
- *Creating A Business and Personal Legacy* by Mark J. Munoz
- *Innovative Selling* by Eden White
- *Present! Connect!* by Tom Guggino
- *Introduction to Business* by Patrice Flynn
- *Be Different!* by Stan Silverman

Announcing the Business Expert Press Digital Library

Concise e-books business students need for classroom and research

This book can also be purchased in an e-book collection by your library as

- a one-time purchase,
- that is owned forever,
- allows for simultaneous readers,
- has no restrictions on printing, and
- can be downloaded as PDFs from within the library community.

Our digital library collections are a great solution to beat the rising cost of textbooks. E-books can be loaded into their course management systems or onto students' e-book readers.
The **Business Expert Press** digital libraries are very affordable, with no obligation to buy in future years. For more information, please visit **www.businessexpertpress.com/librarians**. To set up a trial in the United States, please email **sales@businessexpertpress.com**.

CPSIA information can be obtained
at www.ICGtesting.com
Printed in the USA
BVHW050206070821
613352BV00006B/142

9 781637 420225